WILTON

Tiered Cakes

A SHOWCASE OF
DRAMATIC DESIGNS
FOR SPECIAL OCCASIONS

Dear Friend,

Life's biggest moments usually include a tiered cake. At weddings, baby showers and other milestone events, the cake is at the center of the celebration. For many of these celebrations, a Wilton tiered cake is there, adding to the excitement. Wilton cake designs capture the moment perfectly, using the latest colors, shapes and accents.

Wilton Tiered Cakes continues our tradition of groundbreaking design. In this book, you will see dramatic new color combinations such as our wedding trio of yellow, pink and green. You will discover great ideas for fondant decorating, including a textured stucco look and an amazing jack-in-the-box cake for baby showers. Throughout *Wilton Tiered Cakes*, there are exciting details to inspire you. From color flow champagne bubbles to fondant strips in ice cream colors, every cake features memorable design elements that will set your celebration apart.

And the excitement is not only in the latest cake designs, but in the innovative new products which bring a fresh look to classic tiered cake styles. Look at our cover cake, "Pearl Necklace", and notice how the tiers are separated by globes rather than by traditional upright pillars. The round shape is an exciting change of pace. It's a great look that picks up the shape of the pearl-look fondant garlands and the puffed bow on top.

Elsewhere, you'll see a different approach to rounded construction. We've used a unique see-through globe separator at the center of a fun duck baby shower cake and a beautiful white wedding cake. The gently curving separator is the perfect partner for the shower cake's fondant umbrellas and the wedding cake's icing arches.

Fabric accents are another major story in *Wilton Tiered Cakes*. Traditionally, fabric is used around or under a cake—we've made it part of the cake construction with our wrapped pillars and separators. To see what excitement fabric can bring, look at our "Petal Poetry" design. It's built on our Tailored Tiers set, which is covered with a vine patterned fabric that complements the flower vines on each tier. What a terrific way to extend the theme of your cake.

You'll find everything you need to achieve these amazing cakes inside this book—step-by-step instructions, construction tips, recipes, patterns and great Wilton products. Turn to the great variety of styles in *Wilton Tiered Cakes* to spark your imagination when planning your next big event.

Vince Naccarato

Vince Naccarato
Chairman and CEO
Wilton Industries, Inc.

Credits

Creative Director
Daniel Masini

Art Director/Cake Designer
Steve Rocco

Decorating Room Supervisor
Mary Gavenda

Senior Cake Decorator
Susan Matusiak

Cake Decorators
Debbie Friedman
Ana Johnson
Diane Knowlton
Mark Malak
Tracey Wurzinger
Judy Wysocki

Editor/Writer
Jeff Shankman

Writers
Marcia Adduci
Mary Enochs
Marita Seiler

Copy Editor
Jane Mikis

Production Manager
Challis Yeager

Associate Production Manager
Mary Stahulak

Graphic Design/Production
Marek/Janci Design
Quebecor World Premedia

Photography
Peter Rossi—PDR Productions
Dale DeBolt Photography
BlackBox Studios

Photo Stylist
Carey Thornton

Administrative Assistant
Sharon Gaeta

Product Development/Publications
Sandie Santoro
Tina Celeste

In U.S.A.
Wilton Industries, Inc
2240 West 75th Street
Woodridge, IL 60517

Retail Customer Orders:
Phone: 800-794-5866
Fax: 888-824-9520
Website: www.wilton.com

Class Locations:
Phone: 800-942-8881
www.wilton.com

In Canada
Wilton Industries, Canada, Ltd.
98 Carrier Drive
Etobicoke, Ontario M9W 5R1 Canada

Retail Customer Orders:
Phone: 416-679-0790
Fax: 416-679-0798

Class Locations:
Phone: 416-679-9790, x200
E-mail: classprograms@wilton.ca

¡Se Habla Espanol!
Para mas informacion,
Marque 800-436-5778

Table of Contents

Love Stories p. 4

Create a happy ending with a cake design that expresses your love. See a spectacular garden terrace design built with lattice fence sections, candy plaques and roses all around. Experience a lovely fountain-inspired cake, with cascades of gum paste arches. Or go chocolate—our rich mocha-iced tower is studded with candy panels and a dipped monogram.

Events to Remember p. 32

Discover the perfect wedding shower or anniversary theme here. From a lovebird's nest to an anniversary family photo gallery, you'll find the perfect cake to wow your guests. Try a fun new way to celebrate—serve individual shower cupcakes, each sprouting a color flow blossom and placed on our 3-level cake stand.

Happy Baby p. 40

Give the mother-to-be an unexpected treat—an adorable cake with a 3-D mama duck on top and a procession of fondant ducklings on the hexagon tier below. See many favorite baby themes with some new twists, including Noah's ark, teddy bears and a fun jack-in-the box.

Creating Tiered Cakes p. 48
Learn how tiered cakes are baked and built in this easy-to-use guide. Includes wonderful cake and icing recipes, preparation tips, construction steps and guides for transporting, cutting and serving your cake.

Cake Instructions p. 64
How to decorate each cake in this collection. Includes construction method used and a convenient product checklist.

Special Techniques p. 102
See featured flowers, bows, fondant decorations and other special accents used on our cakes. Each includes close-up views and easy-to-follow instructions.

Tiered Cake Products p. 114
From bakeware and separators to stands and accents, here is a sampling of the innovative Wilton products you need to create our featured cakes.

Keeping in Touch with Wilton p. 128
Be up to date with every cake! A quick look at where to find fun decorating classes and useful product news, how to order from Wilton and more.

Love Stories

Every wedding tells a story. On the cakes that follow, your version

of boy meets girl can be expressed with the romance of a rose,

the fairy tale charm of icing tiaras or the sophisticated sparkle of

champagne bubbles. Make the tale bold and dramatic or sweetly

sentimental. Mix in elegant detail like the cornelli lace here, or keep

it simply iced and surrounded by flowers. As long as you convey

what is in your hearts, it's a story that's sure to captivate your guests.

Shown: *Lace Flair*; instructions p. 64.

Color Harmony

A Rainbow of Romance

Two cakes take divergent multicolor approaches—proof that unusual shades can set just the right tone for informal receptions. Each design can be customized to the specific palettes of invitations, flowers and dresses. Above, *Color Harmony* uses soft pastel bands of cornelli lace to add interest to each tier and the spectacular top bow. At right, *Brilliant Future* showcases vibrant royal icing hearts and scrolls that seem to spring out from the cake tops, for a look with incredible energy. *(Instructions: Color Harmony, p. 65; Brilliant Future, p. 66)*

Brilliant
Future

Love Tops the Tiers

The traditional topper steps aside for a whimsical handcut fondant tiered cake. Lovely cupped flowers and neatly combed cake sides make the point that elegance and fun can share space on the same cake. *(Instructions, p. 67)*

Petal Poetry

Flowers are the language of love, and these blushing blossoms speak to the heart. Adding to the romance, our fabric-wrapped separators carry on the tiers' motif of graceful icing vines. The separators may be easily tailored to your taste using their included acetate wraps to add ribbon, wrapping paper or fabric in your wedding colors and designs.

(Instructions, p. 68)

A Rainbow of Roses

Choose the soothing colors of nature's flowers for a spring or summer garden wedding or to spread sunshine throughout the reception hall in any season.

These blossoms are actually handmade of paper, and are easily tinted with pastel chalk to suit any décor.

(Instructions, p. 69)

Sparkling Tribute

This cool, frosty look will dazzle in winter or summer. Glistening sugar crystals coat mint green fondant tiers which are encircled by lush paper roses and leaves in pure white.

The shimmering silvertone monogram topper completes the arctic effect. Consider this refreshing cake for showers, anniversaries and other special events. *(Instructions, p. 70)*

Stucco Trio

Gracefully suspended, heart-shaped fondant tiers are sponged with icing for a textured effect that's so unique for a wedding.

Adding spark to the stucco-inspired backdrop are gatherings of deep red gum paste fantasy flowers, suggesting a perfect design for autumn celebrations. Change the flower colors and textured fondant canvas to match any season or color theme and you have a blueprint for decorating versatility.

Like the bride, the heart tiers are dressed in special jewelry for the day. Strands of pearl beads are coiled around ropes of fondant and then wrapped around the cake bases, giving each tier its own necklace border as an elegant finishing touch. *(Instructions, p. 71)*

This cake will make the wedding couple feel like royalty...each tier has the look of a bridal tiara. The jewels in each crown are royal icing loops covered with tiny blossoms that echo the side garlands.

(Instructions, p. 72)

Gentle Curves

Like individual wedding bands, ribbed arches of icing encircle this cake, giving it a lovely, airy look. The unique fluted separator continues the curved story between tiers. The clear bowl may be used to showcase fresh or silk flowers, wedding fabric or other decorative touches that enhance white-on-white or floral themes.

(Instructions, p. 73)

Belle of the Ball

Elegant pearl-look separators bring a beautifully-textured display full circle. The smooth fondant-covered tiers create an ideal backdrop for the large and small balls, which dance from bottom to top. If you love the classic grace of an all white cake, stated more boldly, this is the design for you.

(Instructions, p. 74)

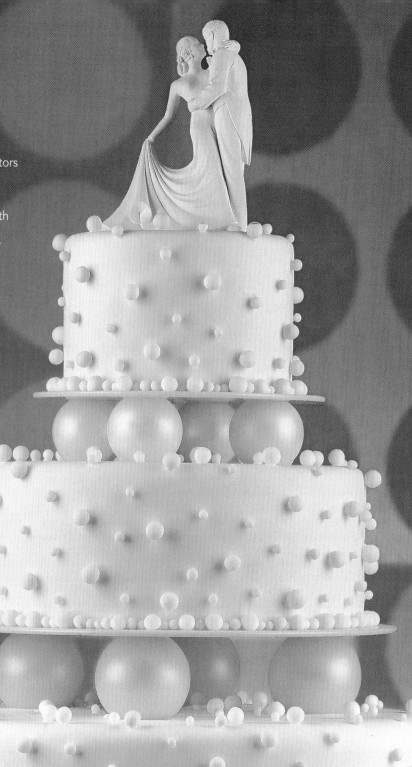

Sparkling Champagne

This calls for a toast: To the effervescent color flow bubbles, the contrasting oval tiers in ivory and white, the magnificent handmade paper bow — and to the bride and groom who choose this exciting signature look for their big day.

(Instructions, p. 73)

Mega Mocha

Definite eye candy. A glistening chocolate tower is framed by candy curves studded with the tuxedo-like touches of candy clay buttons and zigzags. Even the monogram topper is dipped in candy. The taste is as rich as the look, each tier filled with luscious mocha cream (p. 50). Great for the groom's cake — but if your guests crave chocolate, you'll want to have enough to serve everyone. *(Instructions, p. 76)*

Neapolitan Charm

Embossed fondant stripes in a variety of ice cream colors combine with deep, dark chocolate tiers for a triple dip of texture, flavor and fun. Square cakes are set off beautifully by fondant-wrapped globe separators and tiny scoops of fondant at the top borders. *(Instructions, p. 77)*

Garden Terraces

The popular rose garden theme reaches a breathtaking new plateau. A cluster of round base tiers, topped with hexagon candy plaques and framed by lattice icing trellises, begins this remarkable tiered arrangement.

Real roses peek from the base, icing rosebuds on vines climb every tier—even the separators are blooming with floral beauty. Using the clear acetate band included with our fabric-wrapped separators, it's easy to insert colorful rose wrapping paper to complement the bridal theme.

The trellises provide a wonderful openwork element that helps every level work together. They're easy to make in advance, using royal icing and the pattern on p. 104. They

are attached to the sides of each candy plaque at the reception after the cake is assembled.

(Instructions, p. 78)

Roses Upon Roses

Tiers that stand apart pull together a romantic look of hearts and flowers in whisper-soft pink. The tri-level stand enhances the effect of graceful motion.

(Instructions, p. 79)

*Retro
Romance*

A cake that shimmers with style. Sugar coated tiers and soft rolled fondant roses are contrasts in texture that lend a sophisticated touch to this pure white design. The classic couple topper gives it a fun, slightly nostalgic twist.

(Instructions, p. 80)

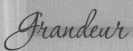

Grandeur

Imagine a spectacular fountain, holding honeymoon wishes for the wedding couple. That is the inspiration for this elegant fondant design. Cascading arches, fashioned from gum paste and decorated with icing scrolls and fondant bows, create the irresistible flowing illusion. Lovely fondant drapes and gum paste rose bouquets complete the dramatic effect.

(Instructions, p. 81)

Full-Bloom Beauty

Fondant-covered tiers are wrapped in ribbon and framed with real roses, for an elegant wedding cake that's beautifully simple in design. Match bands of ribbon or lace to embellishments on the bride's gown and choose fresh flowers that are in her bouquet for a mirror image of her big day. *(Instructions, p. 82)*

Pearl Peaks

Five tiers tall, this cake also makes an impression for its pretty, traditional details. In place of piped drop strings, pearl garlands link together around each tier like accents on a wedding dress, each point marked by an apple blossom. The sweet lovebirds topper has the height needed to complete this towering presentation. This cake is compatible with any size event—just subtract tiers as needed.

(Instructions, p. 83)

Top Moment

Throw a curve at traditional square tiers. We've used

swirling royal icing scrolls to define the sides and surround

the figurine base on a cake perfect for smaller receptions.

(Instructions, p. 84)

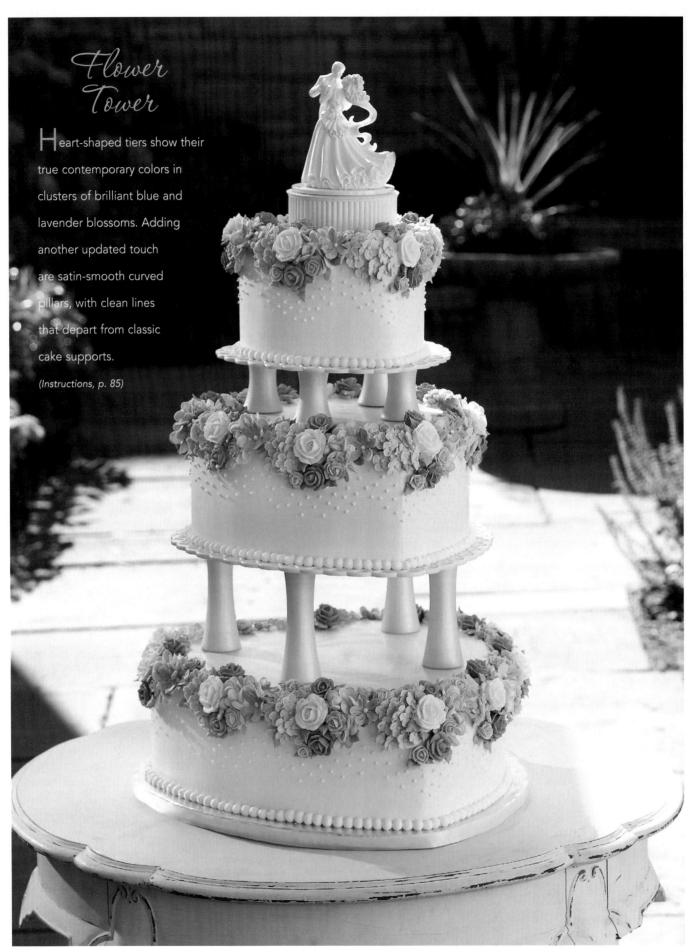

Flower Tower

Heart-shaped tiers show their true contemporary colors in clusters of brilliant blue and lavender blossoms. Adding another updated touch are satin-smooth curved pillars, with clean lines that depart from classic cake supports.

(Instructions, p. 85)

Daisy Chain

Pure fun, powerful colors —
perfect for spring or summer
weddings, outside or in. Perky
Fondant daisies drift around
the borders and cover the
pillars while a bouquet spray
looks like it just popped out
of the top. Fondant stripes
in refreshing colors create
fabulous flower stems on the
cake sides. *(Instructions, p. 86)*

Exhilaration

After all the wedding day stress, it's time to let loose at the reception! With its buoyant bubbles of fondant, kicky swirled separators and eyepopping pastel tiers, this cake won't let you forget that weddings are also about having a great time with those you love. *(Instructions, p. 87)*

Pearl Necklace

The perfection of pearls will always be in fashion. Draped in pearl-look fondant garlands and supported by our pearl-finish globe separators, this beautifully rounded design will add sparkle and sophistication to your event. *(Instructions, p. 88)*

Events to Remember

Although most showers and anniversaries are done on a smaller

scale than weddings, you still can serve a dramatic tiered cake sized

for your guest list. The key is that your tiered cake express the fun

and excitement at the heart of these celebrations of love. Look to

designs like our shower love nest cake or anniversary photo tiers

to do just that. Or consider the cupcake blossoms shown here on

A Sprinkling of Fun. Cupcakes offer the versatile serving option

of a specially-decorated dessert for each guest.

Shown: *A Sprinkling of Fun*; instructions p. 89.

Weather It Together

A gentle drizzle of hearts in a rainbow of pastels makes this the ideal cake to build a shower color scheme around. Wrapped pillars in an iridescent dotted pattern pick up the soft shades on the cake. The couple peeks out from under a pretty gum paste umbrella that complements the ruffle bottom border. *(Instructions, p. 90)*

Love's Safe Harbor

Give the classic lovebirds theme a playful new spin—create their love nest by linking cakes on our Tall Tier Stand with lollipop sticks that capture the color flow heart. Place a flock of matching lollipop favors nearby.

(Instructions, p. 91)

A Shower of Hearts

Set off sparks! A cascade of dazzling wired fondant hearts provides all the fireworks any shower could need. The ease of cutting and coloring fondant has made serving tiered cakes a simpler proposition suitable for any celebration. Easy pastel squares with cut-out hearts and dots are all the decorating required to create a cake bursting with excitement.

(Instructions, p. 92)

Perky Petals

A great way to wake up your basic white fondant cake. Embossed, quilted-look lattice creates fabulous texture. A bouquet of wide-open fondant fantasy flowers adds the perfect touch of color. The result is simple sophistication that will be welcome at showers or any special event. Finish the elegant presentation with our sculpted Ceramic Pedestal Cake Stand. *(Instructions, p. 93)*

Years to Treasure

Anniversaries may bring on nostalgia—but the cake needn't. This design freshens up classic elements like drop strings and bluebells by adding elegant Curved Pillars and a sparkling silvertone numeral ornament.

(Instructions, p. 94)

Words to Love By

Tell the story of a lifelong romance. This cake has the warm feeling of a family scrapbook, thanks to your favorite photos and the words which define them. Don't worry about ruining the photos used on the cake—they'll stay protected in the acetate pockets included with our Tailored Tiers separators.

(Instructions, p. 95)

Happy Baby

One great thing about tiers—sometimes the fun can be built right in to the construction. Here, on *Jack Jumps for Joy*, we've turned the pillars into baby bottles using shaped fondant and transformed a simple square cake into a joyful jack-in-the-box. Look ahead for more amazing ideas like an animal-filled ark and a teddy bear-topped play scene—then start looking forward to the shower.

Shown: *Jack Jumps for Joy*; instructions p. 96.

Duck Under Cover

When you're celebrating the mother-to-be, give her a place of honor on the cake. Here, Mama takes Baby Duck under her wing in a sweet family scene—a great way to create more personality for these favorite shower shapes.

The 3-D rubber ducky cake and fondant umbrellas add dimension and fun to an exciting traditional tier set-up featuring our new Fluted Bowl Separator Set.

(Instructions, p. 97)

The Ark Arrives

So cute you'll wish you could save it for the baby! It's an amazing 3-D fondant scene, with a sparkling rainbow arch and rolling waves that stand up on the cake top or flow over the sides. Making this colorful cruise are a boat-load of adorable animals to greet your guests. Each face is easily hand-shaped in rolled fondant. *(Instructions, p. 98)*

Teddy's Ready to Play!

It's a baby's world all buttoned up in one terrific cake. A cuddly teddy bear sits on top and fun baby blocks seem to separate the tiers. Cozy quilted scallops and a galaxy of stars surround each cake. Even with all the colors and shapes bouncing about, the look holds together beautifully.

In place of a traditional cake topper, we've used a cake! It's so much fun to have a big-as-life 3-D teddy for the shower crowd to enjoy. As an added treat, try this cake with a different flavor—our Banana Cake recipe on p. 49 would work very well. (In fact, why not serve a different flavor of cake for each tier!)

The gum paste blocks only look like they're holding up the cakes. They're actually open at top and bottom to let our spiked pillars do their job of support. (What a great way to add a touch of whimsy and color in an unexpected place.)

Don't forget the great detail on the cake sides. The scallops, stars and buttons are all created with rolled fondant—proof that even a cake iced in buttercream can benefit from fondant's bold texture and exciting colors.

Finally, tie the theme together with some wonderful favors. We've made simple tulle puffs filled with pillow mints and topped by our glue-on favor accents. Your guests will love taking home a small part of baby's world. *(Instructions, p. 99)*

Great Anticipation

Height and drama can be easily achieved while keeping tiers to a minimum. The tall handmade fondant carriage and pretty wrapped pillars instantly lift this cake to centerpiece status. The pillars support the look as well as the cake, with a fabric design featuring flowers and dots mimicked by the icing ruffle below.

(Instructions, p. 100)

A Lifetime of Blessings

Combine the serving ease of a sheet cake with the dramatic flair of stacked tiers for a christening cake to remember. With its lovely royal icing flowers and delicate drop strings, this design has a quiet charm ideal for religious receptions. For a boy, a blue background with yellow flowers will work equally well. *(Instructions, p. 101)*

Creating Tiered Cakes

Putting a towering tiered cake together can seem like a high-wire act. How can you stack 50 pounds of cake (up to 5 tiers) without crushing the bottom tier? What can you do to keep a 3-foot high cake, suspended in midair, from tumbling down? How do you transport those perfectly-decorated tiers to the reception hall in one piece?

Fortunately, you don't need a degree in physics to build tiered cakes or possess magical powers to decorate them. Just follow the time-tested methods in this section. We'll show you the most popular ways to construct tiered cakes, including exciting new designs like our Globe Pillar Sets and Fluted Bowl Separator. You'll learn how to prepare the ideal cake for decorating—perfectly even and crumb-free. You'll see how to create many of the icing flowers and decorations featured on cakes in this book, step-by-step. And you'll discover how to safely carry your amazing cake to the celebration, so you can avoid the stress and enjoy the day.

Because a tiered cake should be as thrilling to taste as it is to see, every cake should start with a great recipe. On the following pages, we present recipes that make it easy to surprise the crowd with some wonderful new flavor combinations. Wake up the classic yellow cake with a mouth-watering Lemon Filling. Bring color and flavor to the table with our pretty Strawberry Cake and Strawberry Cream Filling. Don't forget chocolate— the Rich Chocolate Cake filled with Mocha Cream will create a dessert your guests will long remember. You'll also find classic icings for creating beautiful decorations, including royal, buttercream and color flow.

Cake Recipes

You can't go wrong with a white or yellow cake. Each has a nice light flavor, making these the most popular choices for wedding receptions. Today, couples have so many more flavor options for the wedding cake. If you're looking for a delicious change of pace, consider our banana, chocolate or strawberry cake recipes. They're great for groom's cakes and shower desserts as well.

Classic White Cake

3	cups sifted cake flour
1	tablespoon baking powder
$1/2$	cup butter or margarine, softened
$1 1/2$	cups granulated sugar
$1/2$	teaspoon vanilla extract
$3/4$	cup milk
5	egg whites

Preheat oven to 350°F. Spray pans with Bake Easy™ Spray or use Cake Release. In medium bowl, sift together flour and baking powder; set aside. In large bowl, cream butter and sugar with electric mixer until light and fluffy; add vanilla and beat well. Add flour mixture to butter mixture alternately with milk; beat well after each addition. In separate bowl, using grease-free utensils, beat egg whites until stiff but not dry; gently fold into batter.

If batter will be tinted, as on slice shown above, divide batter into equal portions. Add icing color a little at a time, until desired color is reached. Pour batter into prepared pans.

Refer to baking chart, page 63, for baking times and temperatures for specific pans. Cool 10 minutes in pan on rack; remove and cool completely before decorating.

Makes about 6 cups batter.

Yellow Cake

3	cups sifted cake flour
$2 1/2$	teaspoons baking powder
$1/2$	teaspoon salt
$2/3$	cup butter or margarine, softened
$1 3/4$	cups granulated sugar
2	eggs
$1 1/2$	teaspoons vanilla extract
$1 1/4$	cups milk

Preheat oven to 350°F. Spray pans with Bake Easy Spray or use Cake Release. In medium bowl, sift together flour, baking powder and salt; set aside. In large bowl, cream butter and sugar with electric mixer until light and fluffy. Add eggs and vanilla; mix well. Add flour mixture alternately with milk, beating well after each addition. Continue beating one minute. Pour into prepared pans.

Refer to baking chart, page 63, for baking times and temperatures for specific pans. Cool 15 minutes in pan. Gently loosen sides with spatula and remove. Cool completely before decorating.

Makes about 6 cups batter.

Rich Chocolate Cake

2 1/2 cups all-purpose flour
1   teaspoon baking soda
1/2 teaspoon salt
6   squares (6 oz.) semi-sweet chocolate
3/4 cup (1 1/2 sticks) butter, softened
1 1/2 cups granulated sugar
3   eggs
2   teaspoons vanilla extract
1 1/2 cups milk

Preheat oven to 350°F. Spray pans with Bake Easy Spray or use Cake Release. In medium bowl, combine flour, baking soda and salt. In large microwaveable bowl, place chocolate and butter; microwave at High power 2 minutes or until butter is melted. (Mixture can also be melted on top of range in heavy saucepan over low heat.) Stir until chocolate is completely melted. Combine chocolate with sugar in large mixer bowl; beat with electric mixer until well blended. Add eggs, one at a time, and vanilla; mix well. Add flour mixture alternately with milk; beat until well blended and smooth. Pour batter into prepared pans.

Refer to baking chart, page 63, for baking times and temperatures for specific pans. Cool 15 minutes in pan on rack. Gently loosen sides with spatula and remove. Cool completely before decorating.

Makes about 6 cups batter.

Banana Cake

2 1/4 cups all-purpose flour
1   teaspoon baking soda
1/4 teaspoon salt
3/4 cup (1 1/2 sticks) butter, softened
1 1/2 cups granulated sugar
3   eggs
1 1/2 teaspoons vanilla extract
2   ripe bananas, mashed
3/4 cup sour cream

Preheat oven 350°F. Spray pans with Bake Easy Spray or use Cake Release. In medium bowl, combine flour, baking soda, and salt; set aside. In large bowl, cream butter and sugar with electric mixer until light and fluffy. Add eggs, vanilla and banana; mix well. Add flour mixture alternately with sour cream; blend thoroughly but do not overmix. Pour into prepared pans.

Refer to baking chart, page 63, for baking times and temperatures for specific pans. Cool 10 minutes in pan on rack; remove and cool completely before decorating.

Makes about 5 1/2 cups batter.

Strawberry Cake

2 3/4 cups cake flour
2 1/2 teaspoons baking powder
1 1/4 cups granulated sugar
1   cup (2 sticks) butter, softened
4   eggs
1   teaspoon vanilla extract
2/3 cup milk
1   cup thawed frozen sliced strawberries in syrup

Preheat oven to 350°F. Spray pans with Bake Easy Spray or use Cake Release; line pan bottom with parchment paper. In medium bowl, combine flour and baking powder; set aside. In large bowl, cream butter and sugar with electric mixer until light and fluffy. Add eggs, one at a time, and vanilla; mix well. Add flour mixture alternately with milk, starting with the flour; mix well. Fold in strawberries. Pour into prepared pans.

Refer to baking chart, page 63, for baking times and temperatures for specific pans. Cool 15 minutes in pan on rack. Gently loosen sides with spatula and remove. Cool completely before decorating.

Makes about 6 cups batter.

Icing Recipes

Decorators rely on certain icings to achieve specific effects. Usually an icing's texture is the key element in its selection. For wedding cakes, rich and creamy buttercream is the most popular icing used to cover tiers, along with royal icing for decorations which dry hard and last indefinitely. Rolled fondant is also a favorite; its dough-like consistency is ideal for covering cakes with a smooth satiny surface. Fondant can also be used to hand-shape beautiful 3D flowers and create fun cut shapes and designs. The recipes below and on page 50 are easy to make and the textures can be easily adjusted for your decorating needs.

Buttercream Icing

1/2 cup butter or margarine*
1/2 cup solid vegetable shortening
1   teaspoon Wilton Clear Vanilla Extract
4   cups sifted confectioner's sugar (about 1 lb.)
2   tablespoons milk**

Cream butter and shortening with electric mixer. Add vanilla. Gradually add sugar, one cup at a time, beating well on medium speed. Scrape sides and bottom of bowl often. When all sugar has been mixed in, icing will appear dry. Add milk and beat at medium speed until light and fluffy. Keep bowl covered with a damp cloth until ready to use. For best results, keep icing bowl in refrigerator when not in use. Refrigerated in an airtight container, this icing can be stored 2 weeks. Rewhip before using.

This recipe will yield 3 cups of medium-to-stiff consistency icing. If you'd like to save the time and mess of preparing your own icing, try Wilton Ready-To-Use Decorator Icings (p. 127). Our White Creamy Decorator Icing has a thin-to-medium consistency that's great for spreading, making borders and messages; available in a convenient 5 lb. tub. Our Decorator White and Chocolate Icings are the ideal stiff consistency for making roses and flowers with upright petals; available in 1 lb. cans; may be thinned for icing cakes by mixing in approximately 2 teaspoons water.

Substitute all-vegetable shortening and 1/2 teaspoon Wilton No-Color Butter Flavor for pure white icing and stiffer consistency.

**Add 2 more tablespoons light corn syrup, water or milk per recipe to thin for icing cake.*

Chocolate Buttercream Icing

Prepare Buttercream Icing recipe above.

Add 3/4 cup cocoa (or three 1 oz. unsweetened chocolate squares, melted) and an additional 1 to 2 tablespoons milk to Buttercream Icing recipe. Mix until well blended.

Chocolate Mocha Icing: Substitute freshly brewed strong coffee for milk in recipe.

Darker Chocolate Icing: Add 4 more unsweetened chocolate squares (or 1/4 cup sifted cocoa powder) and 1 more tablespoon of milk to Chocolate Buttercream Icing.

Royal Icing

3 tablespoons Wilton Meringue Powder
4 cups sifted confectioner's sugar (about 1 lb.)
6 tablespoons water*

Beat all ingredients at low speed for 7-10 minutes (10-12 minutes at high speed for portable mixer) until icing forms peaks.

Makes 3 cups.

When using large countertop mixer or for stiffer icing, use 1 tablespoon less water.

Icing Recipes

Rolled Fondant

If you want to save the time and mess of preparation, use Wilton Ready-To-Use Rolled Fondant, p. 125. This perfectly-textured fondant gives you great results without mixing.

1   tablespoon plus 2 teaspoons unflavored gelatin
1/4   cup cold water
1/2   cup Wilton Glucose
2   tablespoons solid vegetable shortening
1   tablespoon Wilton Glycerin
8   cups sifted confectioner's sugar (about 2 lbs.)
    Icing color and flavoring, as desired

Combine gelatin and cold water; let stand until thick. Place gelatin mixture in top of double boiler and heat until dissolved. Add glucose, mix well. Stir in shortening and just before completely melted, remove from heat. Add glycerin, flavoring and color. Cool until lukewarm. Next, place 4 cups confectioner's sugar in a bowl and make a well. Pour the lukewarm gelatin mixture into the well and stir with a wooden spoon, mixing in sugar and adding more, a little at a time, until stickiness disappears. Knead in remaining sugar. Knead until the fondant is smooth, pliable and does not stick to your hands. If fondant is too soft, add more sugar; if too stiff, add water (a drop at a time). Use fondant immediately or store in airtight container in a cool, dry place. Do not refrigerate or freeze. When ready to use, knead again until soft. This recipe makes approximately 36 oz., enough to cover a 10 x 4 in. high cake.

Extra-Firm Rolled Fondant

Use this recipe for a fondant with the extra body and pliability ideal for making drapes, swags, woven and elaborate decorations.

1 to 2 teaspoons Wilton Gum-Tex™
24 oz. Wilton Ready-To-Use Rolled Fondant

Knead Gum-Tex into fondant until smooth. Store in an airtight container or tightly wrapped in plastic.

Thinned Fondant Adhesive

Use this mixture when attaching dried fondant to other fondant decorations or for attaching freshly-cut fondant pieces to lollipop sticks or florist wire.

1   oz. Wilton Ready-To-Use Rolled Fondant (1 1/2 in. ball)
1/4   teaspoon water

Knead water into fondant until it becomes softened and sticky. To attach a fondant decoration, place mixture in decorating bag fitted with a small round tip, or brush on back of decoration. Recipe may be doubled.

Apricot Glaze

Ideal for preparing a cake for fondant or for crumb-coating cakes before icing.

1 cup apricot preserves

Heat preserves to boiling, strain. Brush on cake while glaze is still hot. Let dry. Glaze will dry to a hard finish in 15 minutes or less. Makes enough to cover a 10 x 4 in. cake.

Color Flow Icing
(full-strength for outlining)

1/4   cup + 1 teaspoon water
4   cups sifted confectioner's sugar (about 1 lb.)
2   tablespoons Wilton Color Flow Mix

With electric mixer, using grease-free utensils, blend all ingredients on low speed for 5 minutes. If using hand mixer, use high speed. Color flow icing "crusts" quickly, so keep bowl covered with a damp cloth while using. Stir in desired icing color.

Makes about 2 cups color flow icing.

Thinned Color Flow

In order to fill in an outlined area, the recipe above must be thinned with 1/2 teaspoon of water per 1/4 cup of icing (just a few drops at a time as you near proper consistency). Use grease-free spoon or spatula to stir slowly. Color flow is ready for filling in outlines when a small amount dropped into the mixture takes a count of ten to disappear.
Note: Color flow designs take a long time to dry, so plan to do your color flow piece up to 1 week in advance.

Cake Filling Recipes

When choosing a filling, keep in mind what a cake filling should do. It should not only hold the layers together and keep the cake moist, but also add texture, contrast, color and flavor.

You may use buttercream or chocolate buttercream icing to fill cakes, but not royal icing. For a quick and easy filling, you can also use any flavor of jam or fruit preserves.

Pastry Cream Filling

6   tablespoons granulated sugar
3   tablespoons all-purpose flour
1/2   teaspoon salt
1   cup half & half
4   egg yolks
1   teaspoon vanilla extract

In small saucepan, blend all ingredients, except vanilla, using wire whisk. Heat over medium heat stirring constantly until mixture is thickened, about 5 minutes. Remove from heat; stir in vanilla. Cool before filling cake layers. To prevent a skin from forming, brush with melted butter. Stir before using.

Makes about 1 1/2 cups filling

Chocolate Cream Filling

Prepare Pastry Cream Filling recipe above. Add 2 squares (2 oz.) unsweetened chocolate, melted, when stirring in vanilla.

Mocha Filling

Prepare Chocolate Cream Filling above, reducing the amount of half & half by 2 tablespoons. Substitute 2 tablespoons extra-strong prepared coffee.

Lemon Filling

1 1/2 cups granulated sugar
1/4 cup cornstarch
1/4 teaspoon salt
1 1/2 cups cold water
4 egg yolks, lightly beaten
2 teaspoons grated lemon peel
1/2 cup fresh lemon juice (about 2 medium lemons)
2 tablespoons butter or margarine

In small saucepan, combine sugar, cornstarch and salt. Gradually add water and whisk until well blended. Whisk in egg yolks, lemon peel and lemon juice. Cook over medium heat, whisking constantly, until thick and bubbly. Continue heating 1 minute; remove from heat. Stir in butter. Cool to room temperature, without stirring.

Makes about 2 cups filling.

Strawberry Cream Filling

1 package (15-16 oz.) frozen sliced strawberries in syrup, thawed
1 cup heavy cream
2 tablespoons cornstarch

In medium saucepan, combine strawberries, cream and cornstarch. Cook over medium heat, whisking constantly, until thickened, about 8-10 minutes. Remove from heat. Chill before filling cake layers.

Makes about 2 1/2 cups filling.

Raspberry Cream Filling

Prepare Strawberry Cream Filling recipe above, substituting 1 package (15-16 oz.) frozen raspberries in syrup, thawed, for strawberries.

Praline Filling

1 cup (2 sticks) unsalted butter, softened
8 egg yolks
2 cups firmly packed brown sugar
1/4 teaspoon salt
1/4 teaspoon maple flavoring
2 cups finely chopped pecans

In medium saucepan, combine butter, egg yolks, brown sugar and salt using wire whisk. Bring to a boil over medium heat, whisking constantly until thickened, about 10 minutes. Remove from heat and stir in maple flavoring and pecans. Cool to room temperature before filling cake layers.

Makes about 2 2/3 cups filling.

Other Recipes

Gum Paste

This clay-like dough dries hard and can be rolled thinner than fondant for finer detail. Meant for decoration only, gum paste is used to make specialty flowers and decorations which should be removed from the cake before serving. Gum paste decorations can be made well in advance of the cake and can be saved long after the event.

1 tablespoon Wilton Gum-Tex
3 cups sifted confectioner's sugar (about 3/4 lb.)
4 tablespoons warm water
1 heaping tablespoon Wilton Glucose
1 cup sifted confectioner's sugar (about 1/4 lb.; save until ready to use)

In a large bowl, mix Gum-Tex into 3 cups confectioner's sugar. Make a well in the center and set aside. Mix water and glucose in a glass measuring cup and blend; heat in microwave on high for about 30 seconds until mixture is clear. Pour into well of 3 cups confectioner's sugar and mix until well blended (mixture will be very soft). Place mixture in a plastic bag and seal tightly; let mixture rest at room temperature for 8 hours or overnight. Knead remaining 1 cup confectioner's sugar into gum paste when you are ready to use it. As you work it in, gum paste will whiten and soften. Makes 1 lb., enough for approximately 50 roses or 100 daisies.

Gum Paste Adhesive

1 tablespoon Wilton Meringue Powder
1 tablespoon water

This easy-to-make "glue" will hold your gum paste flowers and other decorations together. Mix Meringue Powder and water together; add more water if mixture is too thick. Brush on gum paste pieces to attach as needed.

Candy "Clay"

1 package (14 oz.) Wilton Candy Melts®*
1/3 cup light corn syrup

Melt Candy Melts following package directions. Add corn syrup and stir to blend. Turn out mixture onto waxed paper and let set at room temperature to dry. Wrap well and store at room temperature until needed. Candy Clay handles best if hardened overnight.

To Use
Candy Clay will be very hard at the start; knead a small portion at a time until workable. If Candy Clay gets too soft, set aside at room temperature or refrigerate briefly. When rolling out Candy Clay, sprinkle work surface with confectioner's sugar or cocoa (for Candy Clay made with Light or Dark Cocoa Candy Melts) to prevent sticking; roll to approximately 1/8 in. thick. Candy Clay can also be rolled out between waxed paper sheets.

To Tint
White Candy Clay may be tinted using Candy Color or Icing Color. Knead in color until well blended.

To Store
Prepared Candy Clay will last for several weeks at room temperature in an airtight container.

* Brand confectionery coating

Making the Cake

Baking and icing the cakes properly is as important as precise decorating. Your flowers, borders and other designs will look their best when you start on a perfect surface. The baked cake should be a light, golden brown with a level top and straight sides. The iced surface should look smooth as a piano finish, with no peaks or gaps to distract the eye.

Your pursuit of perfection begins with the right equipment for the job. Make sure your baking pans are not warped or pitted. Wilton has a great selection of bakeware in the widest variety of shapes and sizes. They're built to keep their perfect shape and surface through years of use. For torting and icing cakes, we suggest using the Wilton Tilting Cake Turntable or Trim 'N Turn Cake Stand. These essential tools let you rotate the cake for easy icing or slicing.

Before You Bake

Being prepared and organized is essential when creating a tiered cake. To avoid surprises at the reception hall, you'll want to be sure your cake set-up will work without a hitch. This means doing a dry run of your cake construction.

To perform your dry run, get all your construction pieces together—pans, plates, pillars, stand, even the fountain and stairs if your design calls for them.

Now assemble the parts as they will appear on the finished cake. This way you can be sure you have the correct size plates and boards for your cakes and that your stairs or flower holder rings will fit properly in the set-up. This is especially helpful if you have to cut your cake boards for specialty shapes like petals or ovals. You can be certain that you've cut to the right size for the cake.

Baking

Concentrate on three factors when baking and preparing your cakes for decorating:

- **Perfect light golden brown color**
- **Precisely level top and bottom**
- **Smooth, crumb-free surface.**

1. Prepare the pans. Thoroughly grease pans using Wilton Cake Release, applied with a pastry brush. Cake Release eliminates the need to grease and flour pans and releases cakes perfectly, without crumbs. You may also grease pans using Wilton Bake Easy™ Non-Stick Spray or solid vegetable shortening. If using shortening, sprinkle inside the pan with about 2 tablespoons flour and shake so that flour covers all greased surfaces. Turn pan upside down to remove excess flour.

2. Fill the pans. Any cake mix or recipe will work, but for fondant-covered cakes you may want to use a firmer cake, such as pound cake. It helps to clip Wilton Bake-Even Strips on the outside of pan before baking to keep cakes level and reduce cracking or crowning. Pour in the batter, filling pan about 1/2 to 2/3 full. Tap filled pans lightly on a countertop to reduce air bubbles in the batter.

3. Bake cakes on middle rack of a preheated oven for time specified in recipe. To test whether a cake is done, insert a toothpick or cake tester near center and remove. If tip is clean, cake is done. Set cakes in pans on wire racks to cool for 10 minutes. To unmold cake, place a cooling rack against the cake and turn both rack and pan over. Lift pan off carefully; flip back to place on cake board. Let cool at least one hour. Brush off any loose crumbs before icing.

Leveling

Remove any crown which may have formed on your baked cake using a serrated knife or Wilton Cake Leveler. This will result in a perfectly level cake for decorating. Levelers are available in 2 styles. Our small leveler has an adjustable wire which levels and torts cakes up to 10 in. diameter and 2 in. high. Our large leveler has an adjustable knife-like blade which levels and torts cakes up to 18 in. diameter and 3 in. high.

Using The Wilton Cake Leveler
Start with cake on a cardboard cake circle. Measure the height you want to cut from your cake, then position the ends of the cutting wire into the side notches to reach that height. Keep legs of Leveler standing level on work surface and cut into the cake, using an easy sliding motion.

Using A Serrated Knife
Place the cake on a cardboard cake circle, then place on a Wilton Trim 'N Turn Turntable. While slowly rotating the turntable, move the knife back and forth across the top of the cake in a sawing motion to remove the crown. Try to keep knife level, and brush off all loose crumbs which can mix into your icing.

Torting

Add height to your tiers and flavor to your cakes by torting and filling each cake. Torting is simply the process of dividing your cake into horizontal sections. Filling is spread between the torted layers, creating an elegant "sandwich" cake! For a professional look, it's essential to tort cakes evenly. That's why it's important to use an adjustable leveler with the height marked or to mark the cake precisely if cutting with a knife. You may tort a tier to create one or several divisions.

Using The Wilton Cake Leveler
Torting is easily done with the Cake Leveler. Follow the same procedure you use for leveling.

Using A Serrated Knife
Measure cake sides and mark with dots of icing or toothpicks all around. Place one hand on top of the cake to hold it steady and rotate the stand. While slowly turning the cake, move the knife back and forth to cut cake along the measured marks. Repeat for each additional layer.

Filling the Layers

The consistency of your filling makes a big difference in the look of your torted cake. Buttercream or thick-consistency fruit fillings work great; don't use any filling which may spoil or runny fruit fillings which may seep into the cake and discolor it. See our recommended filling recipes on page 51.

1. Starting with the bottom layer, leveled or torted side up, create a dam or circle of icing just inside the edge of the cake. Creating a dam will prevent filling from seeping out when other layers are placed on top. To create the dam, squeeze a circle about 3/4 in. high and 1/4 in. from the outside edge.

2. Fill the dam with your choice of filling.

3. Place the next layer on top, making sure it is level. The weight of the layer will cause the circle of icing to expand just right. Repeat until all layers, except the top, are assembled.

Place the top layer, leveled side down, so the top of the cake is perfectly smooth and level.

Icing the Cakes

When you ice a layer cake, remember—crumbs are your enemy. They'll ruin the perfectly clean look you strive for. The trick to keeping crumbs out of your icing is to glide your spatula on the icing. Never allow the spatula to touch the surface of the cake. Some decorators prefer to "crumb coat" layers by lightly icing the cake first, allowing a light crust to form, then adding a top icing cover.

Using a Spatula

1. Place a large amount of thin consistency icing on the center of the cake top. Spread across the top, pushing toward edges.

2. Cover the sides with icing. Smooth sides first by holding the spatula upright with the edge against the side, slowly spinning your decorating turntable without lifting the spatula from the cake's surface. Return excess icing to the bowl and repeat until sides are smooth.

3. Smooth the top using the edge of the spatula. Sweep the edge of the spatula from the rim of the cake to its center. Then lift it off and remove excess icing. Rotate the cake slightly and repeat the procedure,

starting from a new point on the rim until you have covered the entire top surface.

Smooth the center of the cake by leveling the icing with the edge of your spatula. For easier smoothing, it may help to dip the spatula in hot water, wipe dry, and glide it across the entire surface. Set the cake aside and allow the icing to crust over for at least 15 minutes before decorating. At this point you may also lay Wilton Parchment Paper on the iced cake top and gently smooth with the palm of your hand.

Using a Wilton #789 Icer Tip

1. Trim a 16 in. Featherweight bag to fit tip 789. Fill bag half full with icing. Hold bag at 45° angle and lightly press tip against cake. Squeeze a ribbon of icing in a continuous spiral motion to cover cake top, with last ribbon forcing icing over edge of cake top.

2. To ice the sides, squeeze icing as you turn the cake slowly. Repeat the process until the entire cake side is covered.

3. Smooth the sides and top with a spatula, same as above.

Covering the Cake with Rolled Fondant

To determine the diameter you need to roll fondant for covering your cake: measure opposite sides and top of cake across center; roll out fondant to that size, 1/8 to 1/4 inch thick. For example, an 8 inch, two-layer cake, with two sides each 4 inches, equals 16 inches diameter. For simple, accurate measuring, roll out the fondant on top of Cake Dividing Wheel included in Wilton Cake Dividing Set, or use the Wilton Roll and Cut Mat. Sprinkle surface with confectioner's sugar to prevent sticking. If you're using tinted fondant and want to avoid using confectioner's sugar, you may use a spatula to gently lift up fondant from time to time during rolling.

1. Prepare cake by covering with buttercream icing.

2. Roll out fondant sized to your cake (see above). Roll fondant with rolling pin, lifting and moving as you roll. Add more confectioner's sugar if necessary.

3. Gently lift fondant over rolling pin, or lift with the support of both hands, taking care not to tear it with your fingernails. Position on cake. If tear develops pinch together.

4. Shape fondant to sides of cake with Easy-Glide Smoother. We recommend using the Smoother because the warmth of your hands can affect fondant. Use the straight edge of Smoother to mark fondant at base of cake; trim off using a sharp knife or pizza cutter.

5. Smooth and shape fondant on cake using Easy-Glide Smoother. Beginning in the middle of the cake top, move the Easy-Glide Smoother outward and down the sides to smooth and shape fondant to cake and remove air bubbles. If an air bubble appears, pop it with a pin and smooth area again.

6. Your cake is now ready to decorate.

Covering Larger Cakes with Fondant

In most cases, the smaller the cake, the easier it will be to cover with rolled fondant. However, there is an easy way to position and smooth fondant on cakes that are 12 in. diameter or larger. Follow the steps shown to lift fondant onto the cake without tearing.

1. Cover cake with buttercream icing. Roll out fondant sized to your cake.

2. Slide a large cake circle that has been dusted with confectioner's sugar under the rolled fondant. Lift the circle and the fondant and position over cake. Gently shake the circle to slide the fondant off the board and into position on the cake. Smooth and trim as described above.

Success Tip: *Use the Roll & Cut Mat to roll out your fondant. It's the ideal smooth surface for rolling. Best of all, with the mat's pre-marked circles, it's easy to roll the exact size you need. Whenever you are handling fondant, be sure your hands are clean and dry.*

Tinting Fondant

Tint a small ball or enough to cover a whole cake—the important thing is to add just a little of the concentrated icing color at a time, until you arrive at the exact shade you want. If you'd rather not mix color yourself, Wilton also has pre-tinted fondant in a variety of pastel, primary, neon and natural shades.

1. Roll fondant into a ball, kneading until it's soft and pliable. Using a toothpick, add dots of icing color in several spots.

2. Knead color into your fondant ball; be sure to wear Wilton All-Purpose Decorating Gloves to keep your hands stain-free.

3. Continue kneading until color is evenly blended; add a little more color if needed.

Building Tiers

There are no shortcuts when it comes to building a tiered cake. Remember, the same principles an architect follows when creating a skyscraper should be followed on your cake. The proper supports, such as dowel rods, cake circles/boards and separator plates, must be used in the right places in order to prevent the whole structure from toppling over.

In this section we'll show you eleven construction methods that apply to most Wilton tiered cakes. Don't let the prospect of building a towering group of tiers intimidate you. Even the more involved methods, such as Pillar & Stacked Construction, can be done in a few simple steps. These methods are time-tested—they've been used by Wilton decorators for generations, and you will succeed with them as well.

If you do a dry run of the structure as explained on page 52 ("Before You Bake"), and follow the construction steps faithfully, you will feel confident that your cake will stand securely on the celebration day.

The Importance of Dowel Rods

Dowel rods perform a simple, absolutely necessary function. Inserted into the lower tiers of a cake, they bear the weight of the tiers above. Without dowel rods, tiered cakes would collapse, layers would smash, ornaments and decorations would fall and break.

Plastic or Wood?

Wilton Dowel Rods are available in both plastic and wooden styles. Both types offer food-safe support. The type of dowel rod you choose will generally depend on your preference. However, for a stacked cake, using cardboard cake boards between the tiers, you would want to use wooden dowel rods, which can be sharpened into a point and driven through the board to secure tiers together. Of course, you may reinforce the wooden rods with plastic as well.

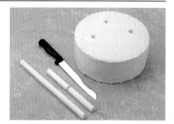

Plastic Dowel Rods are wider in diameter and offer greater stability and more support per dowel rod; therefore, fewer rods need to be used. They are easy to cut to size with a serrated knife, and many decorators prefer their pure white color. They do take up more cake space, and this should be considered when planning the number of servings.

Wooden Dowel Rods are cut easily and cleanly using wire cutters, sharp shears or a small saw. They are economical and strong.

Adding Dowel Rods to Tiered Cakes

Use the upper tier for size reference when determining dowel rod placement. All the dowel rods must be placed within the area you will mark (see steps at right) to provide adequate support.

How Many To Use?

In general, the larger and more numerous the tiers, the more dowels needed. If the tier above is 10 in. or less, use six ¹/₄ in. wooden dowels. Use 8 dowel rods for 16 in. and 18 in. cakes; on these larger tiers, use ³/₄ in. plastic dowel rods in the base tier. When using white plastic dowel rods that are wider and provide more support, the number needed may be less.

1. Center a cake board the same size as the tier above it on base tier and press it gently into icing to imprint an outline. Remove. Use this outline to guide the insertion of the dowel rods*.

2. Insert one dowel rod into cake straight down to the cake board. Make a knife scratch on the rod to mark the exact height. Pull dowel rod out.

3. Cut the suggested number of rods the exact same length, using the mark on the first one as a guide.

4. Now, insert rods into tier, spacing evenly 1¹/₂ inches in from the imprinted outline. Push straight down until each touches the cake board. Repeat this procedure for every stacked or pillared tier on the cake.

Adding Dowel Rods for Ornaments, Flowers or other Decorations

When anything other than regular candles or lightweight toppers is placed on any cake, the area must be reinforced with dowel rods. This prevents crushing of the cake top or the ornament falling off and breaking.

1. Use 3 or 4 dowel rods evenly spaced around a circle approximately the size of the decoration base.

2. Place a cake board or plate on the tier.

3. Position decoration.

Stacked Construction

Stacking is the most architectural method of tiered cake construction. Tiers are placed directly on top of one another and pillars are not used. Cakes are supported and stabilized by dowel rods and cake boards.

1. Dowel rod all tiers except top tier. (see page 55)

2. Position the middle tier on the base tier, centering exactly.

3. Repeat with the top tier.

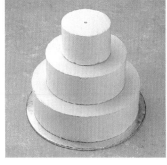

4. To stabilize tiers further, sharpen one end of a wooden dowel rod and push it through all tiers and cardboard cake boards to the base of the bottom tier.

5. To decorate, start at the top and work down.

An Exception—Using Plates to Separate Stacked Tiers

The type of cake sometimes dictates what is placed between the layers for support. Some decorators prefer using separator plates between stacked tiers instead of cake circles when the tiers are heavier than usual (such as fruit cake or dense chocolate cake). This prevents the possibility of the cake circles warping from the excess moisture and weight, thus causing the layers to shift. Of course, if you use separator plates instead of cake circles between the stacked tiers you will not be able to drive a single dowel rod through the stacked tiers for the extra reinforcement as above.

Cake Stand Construction

This is the easiest and safest of all construction methods, because cakes are positioned on plates which fit right into the stand. Each cake stand requires specific cake sizes to fit its design. Many stands come with the plates sized to fit; cake tiers should be 2 in. less in diameter than the plates.

1. Decorate individual cake tiers on separator plates which fit the stand.

2. Position cakes in stand, placing the feet of the separator plate securely inside the bars of cake stand, so that the plate surface rests on the bars.

3. Display the assembled cake on a secure table.

Stands are available in many shapes and styles, making it easy to complement any wedding look. As shown on p. 118 and 119, brides can choose from stands which fit heart, round and square cakes, in contemporary clear acrylic, traditional wrought iron, "floating tiers" and many more styles. The cake stand can also be easily decorated to enhance your cake design. If you have a floral cake, wrap the stand with silk ivy vines or attach silk flowers and greenery. For a pure white cake, you may want to add a dash of color by tying ribbon or tulle puffs on the stand. Or decorate around the stand with taper candles, rose petals and other elegant touches.

Push-In Pillar Construction

Use any type of Wilton Push-In Pillars and Plates. Simple assembly—no dowel rods needed! You may also combine Push-In Pillar with Stacked Construction; this allows you to add fresh flowers, bows or other decorations between the tiers.

1. Mark tier for push-in pillar placement. Use the separator plate for the next tier above, gently pressing it onto the tier, feet down, making sure it is centered. Lift plate away. The feet will leave marks on the icing to guide the position of pillars when you assemble the tier. Repeat this process for each tier, working from largest to smallest tier. The top tier is left unmarked.

2. Place each tier on its separator plate, securing with icing.

3. Position push-in pillars at marks, and insert into tiers. Push straight down until pillars touch the cake board.

4. To assemble, start with the tier above the base tier. Place the feet of the separator plate on the pillar openings.

5. Continue adding tiers in the same way until the cake is completely assembled.

2–Plate & Pillar Construction

Use separator plates and pillars. The most dramatic method of tiered cake assembly—two, three or more single cakes towered together.

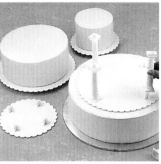

1. Set tiers on separator plates which are 2 in. larger in diameter than cakes.

2. Dowel rod cakes (p. 55) and position separator plates on tiers with feet up. (Note: separator plates connected by pillars must always be the same size in diameter).

3. Position pillars over feet on separator plates.

4. Carefully set cake plate on pillars. Continue adding tiers this way.

Alternate 2-Plate Set-Ups

The Fluted Bowl and Spiral Separator Sets shown here are assembled similar to the 2-Plate and Pillar Construction above— the separators provide support instead of pillars; each set includes 2 separator plates. Cakes must still use dowel rods to support cakes and secure the separators.

Fluted Bowl Separator Set (p. 114)

Spiral Separator Set (p. 115)

Dowel rod base cake as for 2-Plate & Pillar Construction. Position smaller plate from set on base cake (spikes up). Position Fluted Bowl or Spiral Separator over spikes. Position next tier on larger plate from set. Position plate (spikes down) on separator.

2-Plate Pillar & Stacked Construction

The elegance of a stacked presentation, combined with the majestic height of pillar construction. Use any combination of dowel rods, boards, separator plates and pillars. You may also use push-in pillars, which eliminate the need for dowel rods and a plate or board to support the pillars.

1. Mark all tiers for dowel rod placement using a separator plate (for pillar tiers) or a cake circle (for stacked tiers) the same size as the tier above. Insert dowel rods.

2. Position the tier which will be on pillars on a plate 2 in. larger in diameter. The two separator plates which connect the pillars should be the same diameter.

3. Starting at the bottom level, stack tiers. (see p. 56)

4. Position the separator plate (feet up) that will support the tier on pillars.

5. Position pillars over feet.

6. Carefully position the plated tier on the pillars.

Globe Pillar Set Construction

These elegant pearl-look globes are available in separate sets of four 2 in., 2¹/₂ in. or 3 in. globes. The 3 in. globes are to be used to support the base cake only. They have a reinforced center channel which eliminates the need for pillars. The 2 and 2¹/₂ in. sets should be used with 9 in. "Hidden" Pillars (included in set); do not use these sets to support the base cake. Your cake design may use a base board instead of the 3 in. globes to support the base cake as shown here.

1. Position separator plate holding base cake on 3 in. Globe Base Set or a thick base board. Using the separator plate which will hold the cake above, mark base cake for pillar placement (see Push-In Pillar construction, p. 57). Lift plate away.

2. Insert pillars through cake centered over marked area to rest on its separator plate or base board. Place the correct size globe (2¹/₂ in. for cake shown here) over the pillars. Mark pillars where they extend above globes. The cut pillars should be equal to the height of the base cake plus the height of each globe.

3. Trim pillars at markings with craft knife or serrated edge knife.

4. Insert pillars in base cake. Position globes over pillars.

5. Position the tier above on globes.

6. Add additional sets for more tiers.

Tailored Tiers Construction

Our Tailored Tiers Cake Display Set (p. 114) features fabric-wrapped separators which add great texture to your tiered design. The top 2 tiers are decorated on same-size boards, then transported to the reception on larger boards, so that cakes can be easily transferred to the separator plates during assembly. Bottom borders are then added to these tiers. The recommended display for Tailored Tiers separators includes a 14 in. base cake, a 10 in. center cake and a 6 in. top cake.

1. Ice cakes; place 14 in. base cake on 16 in. base board wrapped in foil or 16 in. Silver Cake Base (p. 119). Place 10 in. center and 6 in. top cakes on same size boards. Mark 14 in. and 10 in. cakes for placement of dowel rods. Center the 8 in. plate from the Tailored Tiers set on top of the 14 in. cake and press it gently into icing to imprint an outline. Remove. Use this outline to guide the insertion of dowel rods.

2. Dowel rod 14 in. cake (see page 55). Place the 6 in. plate from set on top of the 10 in. cake and repeat process for marking and inserting dowel rods. Complete decorating on cakes, except bottom borders of 10 in. center and 6 in. top cakes, which will be done at reception. Attach 10 in. and 6 in. cakes to larger boards before transferring to reception.

3. Place the 12 in. plate (spikes up) on table. Center the large (7¼ in.) separator over the plate and press down over the spikes. Position one 8 in. plate (spikes down) on top of the large separator. Place the second 8 in. plate (spikes up) on table. Center the small (4¼ in.) separator over the plate and press down over the spikes. Position the 6 in. plate (spikes down) on top of the small separator.

4. At reception: Position the large separator, with 8 in. plate on bottom and 12 in. plate on top, on the base cake. Remove 10 in. and 6 in. cakes from their larger boards. Position 10 in. cake on large separator.

5. Add bottom border to 10 in. cake. Position the small separator, with 6 in. plate on bottom and 8 in. plate on top, on the 10 in. cake. Position 6 in. cake on small separator. Add bottom border.

To Use Acetate Wrap

1. *Insert photos, patterned paper or fabric in pockets of acetate wrap. Trim inserted items as needed to fit.*

2. *Wrap acetate around separator and fasten Velcro® ends.*

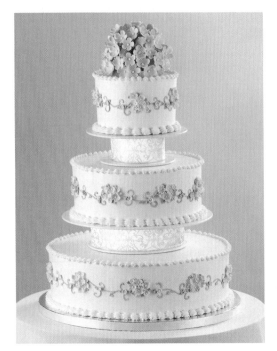

Center Column Construction— Tall Tier Stand

Here's another very easy way to construct a tier cake. The Wilton Basic Tall Tier Cake Stand Set includes 5 twist-apart columns with one bottom and one top bolt, an 18 in. footed base plate, 8, 10, 12, 14 and 16 in. separator plates.

1. Use boards the same size as tiers, or if tiers are shaped, cut boards to fit. Make a waxed paper pattern for each tier except the top tier in order to find the exact center for the columns. Fold the waxed paper pattern in quarters. Snip the point to make a center hole. Test the hole for size by slipping it over a column, adjust size if necessary. Trace hole pattern on prepared cake board and cut out. Also cut a hole in the top tier board to allow for the column cap nut. Save patterns for marking cake tops later.

2. The base tier of the cake will rest on a 14, 16 or 18 in. plate, all of which are included in the Wilton Basic Tall Tier Cake Stand Set. The 18 in. plate is footed; you will need to attach glue-on plate legs (not included) to the 14 or 16 in. plates. To attach legs, turn plate upside down. Using extra-strength glue designed for plastic, attach the six legs, positioning the legs over each of the ribs on the plate.

3. Prepare and ice tiers positioned on prepared cake boards. Make the center holes in two lower tiers for the columns. Mark the top of the cakes with the corresponding waxed paper pattern. Cut the hole by pressing the Cake Corer through the tier right down to the bottom. Hold the corer upright, remove cake corer and push the upper part down to eject the cake center.

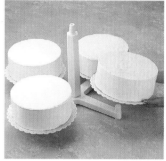

4. Attach a 7¾ in. column to the prepared base plate with the bottom column bolt from underneath the plate. Slip the bottom tier over the column to rest on the plate. Set a plate that is one size smaller than plate below on top of the column.

5. Add a second 7¾ in. column and position the next tier on the plate, slipping it over the column. Finally, add a plate one size smaller than the previous plate, securing with top column nut. Place the top tier on the plate. Mark the backs of all tiers with a dot of icing as a guide when setting up at the reception.

6. To create the "Lady Windermere" look with 4 cakes surrounding the center column, simply replace the footed base plate and its 7¾ in. column with a Wilton Four Arm Base and the 13½ in. column. Insert the four spacers into the openings on the underside of the base at the end of the arms. These spacers will keep the base level once the column and the base bolt are added. Glue the spacers in place. Position four identical base cakes on 10 or 12 in. plates, then add desired tiers upward (up to 3 graduated sizes can be added to the center columns).

Fountain Set-Up with Pillars and Flower Holder Ring

The Wilton Kolor-Flo Fountain, p. 120, easily complements a wide variety of cake designs. Assemble fountain following package directions and test it before the reception for proper water flow. Be sure the display planned will accommodate the height and width of the fountain.

1. Position Flower Holder Ring and Fountain on plate. When using Flower Ring with Fountain, use an 18 in. Decorator Preferred® Scalloped Edge Plate or 17 in. Crystal-Look Plate.

2. Assemble pillars and additional base plate. Use 14 in. or larger plates; 13 in. or taller pillars for the tallest cascade.

3. Assemble cakes.

Transporting the Cake

Moving a tiered cake from one location to another does not have to be difficult. It can be quite easy! Following some simple guidelines ensures that your cake will arrive safely—whether you are traveling hundreds of miles or just a few.

Before Moving Cakes

Be certain the cake is constructed on a sturdy base made of three or more thicknesses of corrugated cardboard. Base tiers of very heavy cakes should be placed on a fiberboard or plywood base, 1/2 in. thick.

Cakes on pillars must be transported unassembled. Toppers, candles and ornaments should be removed from cakes when they are being moved.

For stacked cakes, move the entire assembled cake. Or, for a larger quantity of tiers, transport unassembled and assemble at the reception. Be sure to have with you the equipment and icings you will need to finish any decorating needed after assembly at the reception.

For a cake which combines stacked and 2-plate construction, take tiers apart, keeping stacked tiers as units. Boxing the cake makes transportation easier. Not only does it protect the tiers from damage, but it keeps the tiers clean—free from dirt, dust and bugs. Place the boxes on carpet foam or a non-skid mat on a level surface in the vehicle to prevent shifting. Keep the boxes flat; never place on a car seat. Boxed cakes can also be transported in the trunk of the car, except in hot weather, because air conditioning will not reach the trunk area.

It's also important to find out about the reception location before the event. Knowing what to expect when you arrive can make your delivery and set-up so much easier. Call the reception hall a few days before the event to get an idea of the conditions you will encounter there. Ask whether the room is located upstairs or downstairs. Find out what is the best location for bringing the cake into the building. That way you can park in the right place the first time and minimize the distance your cake has to travel from your car. Also ask how far in advance the cake can be set up so that you can plan your day and reduce the stress.

In Pan

Take tiers apart if constructed in Center Column or Push-in Leg method. Leave columns or legs in place. Position the plates on crumpled foil or in shallow pans if they do not sit level. Remove pillars from tier plates; plates stay in position.

In Box

Place the cakes in clean, covered, sturdy boxes that are sized to the base board of each cake. This prevents shifting within the box and possibly crushing the sides of the cake. If the box is too big, roll pieces of masking tape sticky side out and attach to the inside bottom of the box. Position the cake base on top of the tape, securing the base in the box. For taller decorations, prop up box top and sides, secure with masking tape.

On Non-Skid Foam

If tiers cannot be boxed, they can be transported on large pieces of non-skid foam. Place the foam on the floor of the vehicle, then carefully place the tiers centered on each piece of foam. Remove any ornament or fragile decorations before transporting.

At The Destination

Before you bring in the cake from your car, walk the path you will have to travel to the set-up site. Be alert for any bumps along the way and note any tight spaces you will have to maneuver around. Make sure the cake table is level—it's a good idea to bring a level to check this on set-up day.

Request a cart on wheels to move the cake into the reception area. This is easier and safer than carrying by hand. Remove the cakes from the boxes on the reception table by cutting the sides of the boxes and sliding the cakes out. Bring along a repair kit, including extra icing, prepared decorating bags and tips, flowers and spatulas, just in case it is necessary to make any repairs. Once the cake is assembled, take a picture to establish that the cake was in perfect condition when you left it.

Cake Baking and Serving Guides

The charts below are based on baking recommendations from the Wilton Test Kitchen; your results may vary depending on oven performance or altitude in your area. For large cakes, always check for doneness after they have baked for 1 hour.

Serving amounts are based on party-sized portions of 1½ x 2 in. or smaller wedding-sized portions of approximately 1 x 2 in. Cakes from 3 to 6 in. high, baked in the same size pan, would yield the same number of servings because they follow the same pattern of cutting. Cakes shorter than 3 in. would yield half the number of servings indicated for that pan. Number of servings are intended as a guide only.

Icing amounts are very general and will vary with consistency, thickness applied and tips used. Icing amounts allow for top and bottom borders.

3 In. High Cakes (Using 3 In. High Pans)
The figures for 3 in. pans are based on a 1-layer cake which is torted and filled to reach 3 in. high; fill pans ½ full.

PAN SHAPE	SIZE	NUMBER SERVINGS PARTY	NUMBER SERVINGS WEDDING	CUPS BATTER 1 LAYER, 3 IN.	BAKING TEMP.	BAKING TIME MINUTES	APPROX. CUPS ICING TO ICE AND DECORATE
Round	6 in.	12	12	3	350°	35-40	3
	8 in.	20	24	5	350°	55-60	4
	10 in.	28	38	8	325°	65-75	5
	12 in.	40	56	10½	325°	60-65	6
	14 in.	63	78	15	325°	75-85	8
	16 in.	77	100	18	325°	75-85	9
	18 in. Half, 2 in. layer	110*	146*	9**	325°	60-65	10½
	18 in. Half, 3 in. layer	110*	146*	12**	325°	60-65	10½
Sheet	9 x 13 in.	45	65	11½	325°	70-75	5
	11 x 15 in.	60	90	16	325°	80-85	6½
	12 x 18 in.	72	108	20	325°	85-90	8
Square	8 in.	20	32	6½	350°	60-65	4½
	10 in.	30	50	9	325°	65-75	6
	12 in.	48	72	14	325°	65-75	7½
	14 in.	63	98	19	325°	65-75	9½
Contour	7 in.	6	11	3½	350°	45-50	2
	9 in.	11	17	5½	350°	45-50	2½
	11 in.	16	24	8	325°	80-85	3
	13 in.	22	39	13	325°	75-80	4
	15 in.	32	48	16	325°	75-80	5

For pans 10 in. and larger, we recommend using a heating core to insure even baking. Use 2 cores for 18-in. pans.
*Two half rounds. **For each half round pan.

4 In. High Cakes (Using 2 In. High Pans)
The figures for 2 in. pans are based on a 2-layer, 4 in. high cake. Fill pans ½ to ⅔ full.

PAN SHAPE	SIZE	NUMBER SERVINGS PARTY	NUMBER SERVINGS WEDDING	CUPS BATTER 1 LAYER, 2 IN.	BAKING TEMP.	BAKING TIME MINUTES	APPROX. CUPS ICING TO ICE AND DECORATE
Round	6 in.	12	12	2	350°	25-30	3
	8 in.	20	24	3	350°	30-35	4
	9 in.	24	32	5½	350°	30-35	4½
	10 in.	28	38	6	350°	35-40	5
	12 in.	40	56	7½	350°	35-40	6
	14 in.	63	78	10	325°	50-55	7½
	16 in.	77	100	15	325°	55-60	9
Square	6 in.	12	18	2	350°	25-30	3½
	8 in.	20	32	4	350°	35-40	4½
	10 in.	30	50	6	350°	35-40	6
	12 in.	48	72	10	350°	40-45	7½
	14 in.	63	98	13½	325°	45-50	9½
	16 in.	80	128	15½	325°	50-55	11
Heart	6 in.	8	14	1½	350°	25-30	3½
	8 in.	18	22	3½	350°	30-35	4½
	9 in.	20	28	4	350°	30-35	6
	10 in.	24	38	5	350°	30-35	8½
	12 in.	34	56	8	325°	45-50	9
	14 in.	48	72	10	325°	45-50	10
	15 in.	50	74	11	325°	40-45	11
	16 in.	64	94	12½	325°	40-45	12
Petal	6 in.	6	8	1½	350°	25-30	4
	9 in.	14	18	3½	350°	35-40	6
	12 in.	38	40	7	350°	35-40	9
	15 in.	48	64	12	325°	50-55	11
Hexagon	6 in.	10	12	1¾	350°	30-35	3
	9 in.	20	26	3½	350°	35-40	5
	12 in.	34	40	6	350°	40-45	6
	15 in.	48	70	11	325°	40-45	9
Oval	7¾ x 5⅝ in.	9	13	2½	350°	25-30	3
	10¾ x 7⅞ in.	20	26	5	350°	25-30	4
	13½ x 9⅞ in.	30	45	8	350°	35-40	5½
	16½ x 12⅜ in.	44	70	11	325°	40-45	7½
Sheet	7 x 11 in.	28	32	5½	350°	30-35	5
	9 x 13 in.	45	50	7	350°	35-40	6
	11 x 15 in.	60	74	11	325°	35-40	8
	12 x 18 in.	72	98	14	325°	45-50	10

General Cake Cutting Guides
The diagrams below will give you a general plan for cutting the most popular cake shapes. They will help you serve more attractive, uniform pieces while reaching your targeted number of servings. Diagrams show only one size in each shape; you will use the same general technique to cut each size cake in that shape.

Wedding Cakes—1 x 2 in. slices
The diagrams show how to cut popular shaped wedding tiers into slices approximately 1 x 2 in. and 2 layers high (about 4 in.) For cakes shorter than 3 in. you will need to cut wider slices to serve a proper portion; even if a larger serving size is desired, the order of cutting is still the same. Before cutting the cake, remove the top tier, which is usually saved for the first anniversary and is not included in our serving amounts for wedding cakes in this book. Begin by cutting the 2nd tier, followed by the 3rd, 4th and so on.

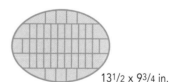
13½ x 9¾ in.   12 in.

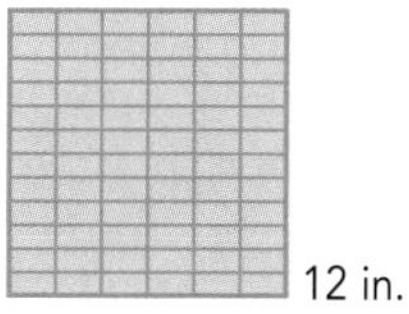

Oval Tiers: Move in 2 in. from the outer edge and cut across. Slice and serve 1 in. pieces of cake. Now move in another 2 in., repeat process until the entire tier is cut.

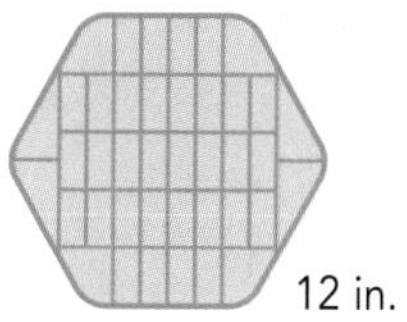

Hexagon Tiers: Move in 2 in. from the outer edge and cut across. Slice and serve 1 in. pieces of cake. Now move in another 2 in., repeat process until the entire tier is cut.

12 in.

Square Tiers: Move in 2 in. from the outer edge and cut vertically, top to bottom. Slice and serve 1 in. pieces of cake. Now move in another 2 in. and repeat process until the entire tier is cut.

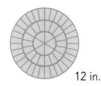
12 in.

Round Tiers: Move in 2 in. from the tier's outer edge and cut a circle. Slice and serve 1 in. pieces from around the circle. Now move in another 2 in. and cut another circle. Repeat process until the tier is completely cut. The center core of each tier and the small top tier can be cut into 4ths, 6ths, or more, depending on size.

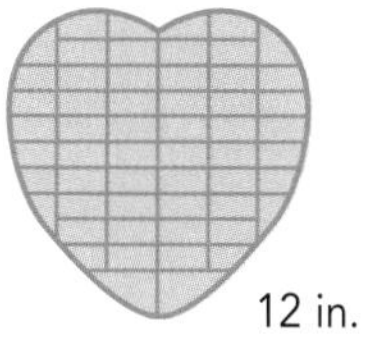

Party Cakes—1½ x 2 in. slices
Follow the diagrams above to cut party cakes (from 3 to 6 in. high), but adjust for the larger party-size slices. For cakes shorter than 3 in. you will need to cut wider slices to serve a proper portion; even if a larger serving size is desired the order of cutting is still the same.

Rounds: To cut round cakes, move in 2 in. from the cake's outer edge; cut a circle and then slice approximately 1½ in. pieces within the circle. Now move in another 2 in. and cut another circle; slice approximately 1½ in. pieces. Continue until the cake is completely cut. Note: 6 in. diameter cakes should be cut in wedges, without a center circle. Cut petal and hexagon cakes similar to round cakes.

Squares: To cut square cakes, move in 2 in. from the outer edge and cut top to bottom, then slice approximately 1½ in. pieces. Now move in another 2 in. and continue until the entire cake is cut.

Sheets: Cut sheet cakes similar to square cakes.

12 in.

Heart Tiers: Divide the tiers vertically into 2 in. wide rows. Within rows, slice and serve 1 in. pieces of cake.

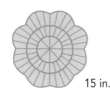
15 in.

Petal Tiers: Cut similar to round tiers as diagram shows.

Lace Flair

from page 4

CONSTRUCTION METHOD:
Stacked, p. 56; Alternate 2-Plate
Construction, p. 58

Pans:
- 8, 12, 16 x 2 in. Rounds, p. 126

Tips:
- 1, 4, 7

Ornament:
- Just Married, p. 121

Also:
- 10 in. and 14 in. Spiral Separator Sets (10 in. includes an 8 and a 10 in. separator plate; 14 in. includes a 10 and 14 in. separator plate), p. 115
- 18 in. Decorator Preferred® Smooth-Edge Separator Plate, p. 117
- Plastic Dowel Rods, p. 120
- Heart Silver Toasting Glasses and Servers Ensemble, p. 123
- 10 in. Round Silver Cake Bases (6 needed), p. 119
- Cake Circles, p. 119
- Fanci-Foil Wrap, p. 119
- Cake Dividing Set
- 10 x 5¼ in. high round craft block
- ½ in. wide white ribbon (16 ft.)
- Silk flowers
- Toothpicks
- Ruler
- Cellophane tape

Cakes Needed:
- 2-layer (4 in. high) 8 in. Rounds (7 needed)
- 2-layer (4 in. high) 12 in., 16 in. Rounds

Recipe:
- Buttercream Icing††, p. 49

Wrap craft block with foil. Ice cakes smooth. Divide 8 in. cakes into 8ths, 12 in. cake into 12ths, 16 in. cake into 16ths. With toothpick, mark 2 in. from top edge of cake at division points. Trace an arc shape from point to point; arc will be 1 in. deep at shortest points. Place 6 of the 8 in. cakes on 10 in. silver cake bases. Prepare these 6 cakes for stacked construction. Position around craft block. Position 18 in. plate over cakes, marking area where 18 in. plate will rest. This area is where dowel rods are needed. Position 8 in. plate on top of 12 in. cake and 10 in. plate on top of 16 in. cake. Cover cake tops and side arc areas with tip 1 sotas. Pipe tip 4 bead borders below each arc design. Add 3 (large, medium, small) tip 7 balls at each arc point, using heaviest pressure for top ball and

decreasing pressure for the remaining 2 balls. Pipe tip 7 ball bottom borders on all cakes. Attach ribbon around the six 10 in. cake bases with tape.

At reception: Position foil-wrapped craft block in center surrounded by 6 of the 8 in. cakes. Position 16 in. cake on top of craft block and partially on 8 in. cakes. Add flowers inside separator stands. Position 12 in. cake on 14 in. separator set using 14 in. plate. Position 8 in. top cake on 10 in. separator set using 10 in. plate. Position remaining flowers. **Serves 300****

64 WILTON TIERED CAKES

CONSTRUCTION METHOD:
Stacked Construction, p. 56

Pans:
- 6, 10, 14 x 2 in. Round, p. 126
- 18 x 3 in. Half Round, p. 126

Tips:
- 1, 3, 5

Colors*:
- Lemon Yellow, Golden Yellow, Rose, Sky Blue, Leaf Green, Violet, Kelly Green

Also:
- White Ready-To-Use Rolled Fondant (288 oz.), p. 125
- Brush Set
- Rolling Pin
- Roll & Cut Mat
- Easy-Glide Fondant Smoother
- Gum Paste Mix
- Meringue Powder
- Piping Gel
- Plastic Dowel Rods, p. 120
- Cake Circles, p. 119
- Fanci-Foil Wrap, p. 119
- 23 x 1/2 in. thick plywood circle
- Cornstarch or confectioner's sugar
- Waxed paper
- 3/8 in. wide white ribbon (6 ft.)
- Cotton balls
- Cellophane tape
- Ruler
- Craft knife

Cakes Needed:
- 2-layer (4 in. high) 6, 10, 14 in. Rounds
- 2-layer (4 in. high) 18 in. Half Rounds (Pan is 3 in. deep, bake 4 half round cakes, 2 in. high, to create a whole 18 x 4 in. round cake)

Recipes:
- Buttercream Icing††, p. 49
- Royal Icing, p. 49
- Gum Paste, p. 50

Several days in advance: Make fondant bow† (p. 102) with 12 loops. Prepare gum paste and combine with 24 oz. fondant. Roll out mixture 1/8 in. thick. Cut 12 strips, 1 x 8 in. Reserve remaining mixture. Fold strips in half and pinch ends together, attaching with damp brush. Let dry overnight, standing on cut side, on board dusted with cornstarch. When dry, using royal icing, pipe tip 1 cornelli lace in assorted colors on loops; edge with white tip 3 balls at top and bottom of each loop. Let dry. For base board, cover plywood board with foil.

Prepare cakes for stacked construction.
Prepare for rolled fondant by lightly icing with buttercream. Cover cakes with fondant; smooth with Fondant Smoother. Mark a 1 in. wide band around the center of each cake, 1 1/2 in. from top and bottom edges. Using royal icing, pipe tip 1 cornelli lace in assorted colors within markings. Edge top and bottom of marked area with tip 3 balls. Add tip 5 ball bottom borders in buttercream on 6, 10 and 14 in. cakes.

Make fondant ruffle (p. 102) for bottom of cake: Roll out reserved fondant/gum paste mixture 1/8 in. thick. Cut 3 x 12 in. strips. Brush

1/4 in. wide line of piping gel on cake board around cake to hold ruffle. Pleat one end of strip and shape ruffle on other side; place pleated side against bottom edge of 18 in. cake. Position cotton balls under ruffles to hold shape. Repeat with remaining strips to encircle cake with ruffles. Tuck cut ends of ruffled strips under to conceal.

Using royal icing, pipe tip 1 cornelli lace on ruffle. Edge ruffle with tip 3 balls. Add tip 5 ball bottom border on 18 in. cake. Remove cotton balls from ruffles. Attach bow loops to cake top with royal icing. Attach ribbon around base board with tape. **Serves 262**.**

Combine Rose with a little Violet for rose shade shown. Combine Lemon Yellow and Golden Yellow for yellow shade shown. Combine Leaf Green and Kelly Green for green shown.

**The top tier is often saved for the first anniversary. The number of servings given does not include top tier.*

†To save time, try our ready-made 6 1/2 in. Cake Bow (p. 116) and decorate to match fondant bow here.*

††Or use Wilton Ready-To-Use Decorator Icing.*

Brilliant Future

from page 7

CONSTRUCTION METHOD:
Push-In Pillar Construction, p. 57

Pans:
- 6, 8, 10 x 2 in. Squares, p. 126

Tips:
- 6, 8

Colors*:
- Rose, Leaf Green, Lemon Yellow, Violet

Ornament:
- Love's Duet, p. 121

Patterns:
- Scroll, Heart, p. 109

Also:
- White Ready-To-Use Rolled Fondant (18 oz.), p. 125
- Heart Cut-Outs™
- Fondant Ribbon Cutter/Embosser Set
- Rolling Pin
- Roll & Cut Mat
- Brush Set
- 7, 9 in. Square Separator Plates, p. 117
- "Hidden" Pillars (2 pks.), p. 116
- 13 x 19 in. Cake Boards, p. 119
- Fanci-Foil Wrap, p. 119
- 6 in. Lollipop Sticks
- Meringue Powder
- Waxed paper
- Plastic straws
- 1/2 in. thick cardboard or foam core board (12 in. square)
- 1/4 in. wide white ribbon (4 ft.)
- Vegetable pan spray
- Cellophane tape

Cakes Needed:
- 3-layer 6, 8, 10 in. Squares (bake two 2 in. and one 1 in. high cake for each 5 in. high tier)

Recipes:
- Buttercream Icing††, p. 49
- Royal Icing, p. 49

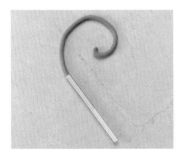

Several days in advance: Make scrolls and hearts using royal icing. Tape several copies of scroll patterns to boards and cover with waxed paper. Spray waxed paper lightly with vegetable pan spray, then wipe off with soft tissue to leave a light coating. Using tip 8, make 40 rose, 48 green and 56 violet scrolls (make extras to allow for breakage); let dry. Repeat process to make 2 rose hearts. When dry, attach lollipop sticks to bottom of hearts with royal icing; let dry.

Prepare cakes for Push-In Pillar Construction. Ice cakes smooth in buttercream. Tint 4 oz. fondant rose, 6 oz. green and 8 oz. violet. Roll out colors 1/8 in. thick. Using wavy edge wheels of Cutter/Embosser with two 1 in. and one 1/4 in. spacers, cut 4 violet strips for 10 in. cake; attach to cake sides with damp brush. Cut 4 green strips for 8 in. cake using one 1 in. spacer and one 3/4 in. spacer; cut 4 rose strips for 6 in. cake using one 1 in. spacer; attach. Using large Cut-Out, cut 2 violet hearts

for each violet strip and attach with damp brush. Cut 3 medium green hearts for each green strip and 5 small rose hearts for each rose strip; attach. Pipe tip 6 ball bottom borders. Cut a straw to 5 in. high for each scroll; pipe a small amount of royal icing in bottom of each straw. Break off a small piece from bottom of each scroll and insert scroll in top of straw; let dry.

At reception: Assemble cakes, placing 10 in. cake on foil-wrapped 1/2 in. thick board. Attach ribbon around base board edge and secure with tape. Insert scrolls into cakes, 1 in. from edge. Position ornament.† Insert hearts. **Serves 82.****

Combine Leaf Green with a little Lemon Yellow for green shade shown. Combine Violet with a little Rose for violet shade shown.

†*Always place a separator plate or cake board, cut to fit, on the cake before you position any figurine or ornament. This protects both the cake and your keepsake. For extra stability, secure your figurine to the plate with double-stick craft tape.*

Love Tops the Tiers

from page 8

CONSTRUCTION METHOD:
Stacked Construction, p. 56

Pans:
Oval Pan Set, p. 127

Tips:
2, 3, 4, 6

Colors*:
Rose, Leaf Green, Kelly Green

Ornament:
Love's Duet, p. 121

Pattern:
Tiered Cake Topper, p. 110

Also:
White Ready-To-Use Rolled Fondant (24 oz.), p. 125

Heart, Flower Cut-Outs™

Rolling Pin

Roll & Cut Mat

Confectionery Tool Set

Icing Sculptor™

Flower Former Set

11³/4 in. Lollipop Sticks

Candy Melting Plate

Cake Circles, p. 119

Fanci-Foil Wrap, p. 119

Dowel Rods, p. 120

Meringue Powder

¹/4 in. wide white ribbon (4 ft.)

Cornstarch

Cellophane tape

Cakes Needed:
2-layer (4 in. high) 7³/4 x 5⁵/8 in. Oval

2-layer (3 in. high) 10³/4 x 7⁵/8 in. Oval

Recipes:
Buttercream Icing††, p. 49

Royal Icing, p. 49

Several days in advance: Prepare fondant flowers, leaves, heart and tiered cake topper. For flowers, tint a 1¹/2 in. ball of fondant rose; roll out rose and white fondant ¹/8 in. thick. Cut 4 rose flowers using small Cut-Out and 55 white flowers using medium Cut-Out. Let dry in melting plate cavities dusted with cornstarch. When dry, using white royal icing, pipe tip 4 dot center in rose flowers and tip 6 dot center in white flowers. Cut out heart from rose fondant using medium Cut-Out. Let dry flat on surface using cornstarch.

dusted with cornstarch. For leaves, tint a 2¹/2 in. ball of fondant green. Roll out ¹/8 in. thick; cut 55 leaves using smallest Cut-Out. Score vein lines using veining tool. Let dry in small Flower Formers dusted with cornstarch. For tiered cake topper, roll out white fondant ¹/8 in. thick; cut out using pattern. Let dry flat on surface dusted with cornstarch.

Decorate tiered cake topper. Using white royal icing, pipe in tip 3 scallop shapes along top tier edges, pat smooth with finger dipped in cornstarch. Using rose royal icing, pipe tip 2 outlines and e-motion details; using white royal icing, pipe tip 2 dots. Let dry. Using royal icing, attach lollipop stick to back, so that stick extends ³/4 in. above top edge of topper. Attach heart to stick with royal icing. Let dry.

Ice cakes smooth in buttercream; ice sides ¹/2 in. thick. Using Icing Sculptor, comb sides using alternating pink and ivory blades. Prepare cakes for Stacked Construction; place base cake

on double-thick, foil-wrapped cake boards. Pipe tip 4 bead bottom borders. Attach flowers and leaves at bottom borders using dots of buttercream icing. Attach ribbon around base board edge with tape.

At reception: Insert topper. Attach rose flowers to bottom edge with dots of icing. Position ornament. **Serves 26.****

*Combine Kelly Green with Leaf Green for green shown.

**The top tier is often saved for the first anniversary. The number of servings given does not include top tier.

††Or use Wilton Ready-To-Use Decorator Icing.

Petal Poetry

from page 9

CONSTRUCTION METHOD:
Tailored Tiers Construction, p. 60

Pans:
- 6, 10, 14 x 2 in. Rounds, p. 126

Tips:
- 2, 3, 16, 20, 349

Colors:
- Moss Green, Rose

Also:
- Tailored Tiers Cake Display Set, p. 114
- 16 in. Round Silver Cake Base, p. 119
- Floral Collection Flower Making Kit
- Confectionery Tool Set
- Flower Formers Set
- Flower Spikes
- Decorator Brush Set
- Cake Dividing Set
- Gum Paste Mix (2 cans)
- Meringue Powder
- Dowel Rods, p. 120
- Cake Circles, p. 119
- 10 in. square craft block
- 22-gauge green cloth-covered florist wire (60 pieces, 8 in. long)
- 24-gauge green cloth-covered florist wire (30 pieces, 6 in. long)
- 1/2 in. wide white ribbon (52 in.)
- Green floral tape
- Wire cutters
- Cornstarch

Cakes Needed:
- 2-layer (4 in. high) 6, 10, 14 in. Rounds

Recipes:
- Buttercream Icing††, p. 49
- Royal Icing, p. 49
- Gum Paste, p. 50
- Gum Paste Adhesive, p. 50

One week in advance: Make flowers and leaves. Prepare gum paste; tint 1/4 green and remainder rose. Roll out green mixture 1/16 in. thick and cut 30 leaves using large rose leaf cutter from Floral Collection Kit. Place on thin foam and vein with small end of veining tool from confectionery set. Turn leaf over and brush center with adhesive, 2/3 from bottom. Press 24-gauge wire in center for stem, pinch bottom of leaf around wire and let dry in craft block. Roll out rose mixture 1/16 in. thick and cut 60 flowers (p. 103) using pansy cutter from kit. Place on thick foam and cup petals with ball tool from set; let dry in small flower formers dusted with cornstarch. Add tip 3 dot centers in royal icing. Follow Violet Stem instructions from Gum Paste Flowers book in kit to make 60 stems on 22-gauge wires. Attach flowers to calyxes with royal icing. Arrange 10 groups of 6 flowers and 3 leaves; tape each group, then arrange in a bouquet and tape groups together. Set bouquet aside. Using rose mixture and cutters from kit, make 144 forget-me-nots and 96 apple

blossoms. Place on thick foam and cup with ball tool. Let dry in small flower formers dusted with cornstarch. Add tip 2 dot centers in royal icing.

Prepare cakes for Tailored Tiers Construction. Ice cakes smooth on same-size cake circles, then attach 6 and 10 in. cakes to larger cake circles for transporting. Divide 6 in. cake into 6ths, 10 in. cake into 8ths and 14 in. cake into 10ths, marking at center of cake sides. Attach 4 apple blossoms and 4 forget-me-nots at division marks with buttercream. Pipe tip 3 vines in buttercream. Attach 2 more forget-me-nots on vines between each mark; add tip 349 leaves. Pipe tip 16 shell top borders. Pipe tip 20 shell bottom border on 14 in. cake.

At reception: Position cakes, removing 6 and 10 in. cakes from larger circles, on assembled Tailored Tiers. Pipe tip 20 shell bottom borders. Position bouquet in flower spike and insert in center of top tier. Tape ribbon to sides of silver cake base. **Serves 116.**

A Rainbow of Roses

from page 10

CONSTRUCTION METHOD:
Stacked Construction, p. 56

Pans:
- 8, 12, 16 in. Rounds, p. 126

Tip:
- 3

Also:
- 12 in. Floral Cake Decorations, p. 122
- White Ready-To-Use Rolled Fondant (180 oz.), p. 125
- Easy-Glide Fondant Smoother
- Rolling Pin
- Roll & Cut Mat
- Brush Set
- Dowel Rods, p. 120
- Cake Circles, p. 119
- Fanci-Foil Wrap, p. 119
- 18 in. round foamcore or plywood board, 1/2 in. thick
- White satin ribbon, 1/2 in. wide (5 ft.)
- Non-toxic pastel chalk (rose, lavender, yellow, green)
- Tea strainer
- Cellophane tape

Cakes Needed:
- 2-layer (4 in. high) 8, 12, 16 in. Rounds

Recipe:
- Buttercream Icing††, p. 49

In advance: Dust rose decorations with chalk. Grate chalk through tea strainer and brush on flowers and leaves; set aside.

For base board, cover foamcore or plywood board with foil. Tape ribbon to side of board. Prepare 2-layer cakes for stacked construction. Prepare for rolled fondant by lightly icing with buttercream. Cover cakes with fondant; smooth with Fondant Smoother. Pipe tip 3 bead bottom borders. Position rose sprays over cakes.
Serves 156.*

*The top tier is often saved for the first anniversary. The number of servings given does not include top tier.

††Or use Wilton Ready-To-Use Decorator Icing.

Sparkling Tribute

from page 11

CONSTRUCTION METHOD:
Stacked Construction, p. 56

Pans:
- 6, 8, 10 x 2 in. Round, p. 126

Colors*:
- Leaf Green, Moss Green

Ornament
- Monogram Picks, p. 122

Also:
- White Ready-To-Use Rolled Fondant (72 oz.), p. 125
- Easy-Glide Fondant Smoother
- Sparkling Sugar (2 pks.), p. 125
- 12 in. Silver Cake Base, p. 119
- 12 in. Floral Cake Decorations (2 pks.), p. 122
- Plastic Dowel Rods, p. 120
- Piping Gel
- Pastry Brush

Cakes Needed:
- 2-layer (4 in. high) 6, 8, 10 in. Rounds

Recipe:
- Buttercream Icing††, p. 49

Prepare cakes for stacked construction.
Prepare cakes for rolled fondant by lightly icing with buttercream. Tint fondant green. Cover cakes with rolled fondant; smooth with Fondant Smoother. Thin 2 to 3 tablespoons of piping gel with water; brush on cakes and immediately sprinkle with Sparkling Sugar. Stack cakes on base. Let set.

At reception: Position rose decorations around cake. Insert monogram picks.
Serves 62.**

*Combine Leaf Green with a small amount of Moss Green for green shown.

**The top tier is often saved for the first anniversary. The number of servings given does not include top tier.

††Or use Wilton Ready-To-Use Decorator Icing.

Stucco Trio
from page 12

CONSTRUCTION METHOD:
Cake Stand Construction p.57

Pans:
- Heart Pan Set, p. 127
- Mini Ball (3 needed), p. 127
- 24 Cup Mini Muffin

Tip:
- 3

Colors:
- Ivory, Red-Red, Golden Yellow, Moss Green

Also:
- Heart Floating Tiers Stand Set, p. 118
- Confectionery Tool Set
- Flower Former Set
- White Ready-To-Use Rolled Fondant (150 oz.), p. 125
- Gum Paste Mix (2 cans)
- Easy-Glide Fondant Smoother
- Heart, Leaf Cut-Outs™
- Rolling Pin
- Roll & Cut Mat
- Fondant Shaping Foam
- Brush Set
- Large (6mm) White Pearl Beading (2 pks.), p. 120
- Meringue Powder
- Cake Boards, p. 119
- Non-toxic pastel chalks
- Tea strainer
- Waxed paper
- Cornstarch

Cakes Needed:
- 2-layer (4 in. high) 6, 10, 14 in. Hearts

Recipes:
- Buttercream Icing††, p. 49
- Royal Icing, p. 49
- Gum Paste, p. 50
- Gum Paste Adhesive, p. 50

At least one week in advance: Make 7 large and 22 medium gum paste flowers (p. 103). Seven of the medium flowers will go inside large flowers to make fantasy flowers.

Also in advance: Make 6 large and 20 medium gum paste leaves. Tint 1/3 can gum paste green. Roll out 1/8 in. thick. Cut leaves using large and medium Cut-Outs. Place on thin foam and score veins using veining tool. Let dry on medium and large flower formers dusted with cornstarch.

Prepare cakes for rolled fondant by lightly icing with buttercream. Tint fondant ivory; cover cakes and smooth with Fondant Smoother. Reserve remaining fondant. To create sponging effect,

dip crushed waxed paper in thinned royal icing and dab onto cakes. For bottom borders, roll reserved fondant into 1/2 in. diameter ropes; twist pearl beads around each rope, about 1 in. apart. For 6 in. cake, make 22 in. rope and use 52 in. long pearl strand; for 10 in. cake make 36 in. rope and use 84 in. long pearl strand; for 14 in. cake, make 48 in. rope and use a 106 in. long pearl strand. Position borders. Attach flowers and leaves with dots of royal icing.

At reception: Position bottom tier, then two top tiers. **Serves 110.****

Love's Legacy
from page 14

CONSTRUCTION METHOD:
Center Column Construction
(Tall Tier Stand), p. 61

Pans:
- 6, 10, 14 x 2 in. Rounds, p. 126
- 18 x 3 in. Half Round, p. 126

Tips:
- 2, 3, 5, 8, 21, 45, 131, 190, 225

Patterns:
- Small and Large Teardrop Loops, p. 111

Also:
- Tall Tier Cake Stand Set (8, 12 and 16 in. Plates, 18 in. Base Plate, three 7³/4 in. columns, Bottom Column Bolt and Top Column Cap Nut needed), p. 119
- Cake Corer Tube, p. 119
- Meringue Powder
- Cake Circles, p. 119
- Fanci-Foil Wrap, p. 119
- 19 x ¹/2 in. thick foamcore board
- Waxed paper
- Cornstarch
- Spatula

Cakes Needed:
- 2-layer (3 in. high) 6, 10, 14 in. Rounds
- 2-layer (3 in. high) 18 in. Half Rounds (bake 4 half round cakes, 1¹/2 in. high, to create a whole 18 x 3 in. round cake)

Recipes:
- Buttercream Icing††, p. 49
- Royal Icing, p. 49

At least one week in advance: Make flowers and teardrop loops. Using royal icing, make 2,000 tip 225 swirl drop flowers with tip 2 dot centers, 65 tip 190 swirl drop flowers with tip 3 dot centers and 130 tip 131 swirl drop flowers with tip 3 dot centers. Make extras to allow for breakage and let dry. For teardrop loops, tape patterns to cake board and cover with waxed paper. Using royal icing and tip 8, outline 65 large teardrop loops and 45 small teardrop loops. Let dry overnight. When dry, attach 7 tip 225 drop flowers to small loops. On waxed paper-covered board, using royal icing, pipe tip 21 rosettes and immediately insert a large loop in center of each, pointed end down. Let dry completely, checking occasionally to be sure that loops remain upright. When dry, using royal icing and starting at top of loop, attach 1 tip 190 drop flower, then 2 tip 131 drop flowers on each side and additional tip 225 drop flowers to bottom of loop. Attach tip 225 drop flowers around rosette base. Let dry.

Prepare cakes and boards for center column construction. For base board, after cutting out center for column, wrap 19 in. foamcore circle with foil. Ice cakes smooth with buttercream. Position 18 in. cake on base board ice exposed top side of board smooth (sides will be iced at reception). Mark all cakes in 2¹/2 in. divisions. From division points, pipe tip 3 drop strings, 1¹/4 in. deep. Immediately attach tip 225 drop flowers to strings. Pipe tip 2 dots below. Pipe tip 5 bead bottom border on all cakes.

At reception: Assemble cakes on Tall Tier Stand. At division points, attach large teardrop loops with tip 8 and buttercream icing. On 18 in. cake, cover side of base board with tip 45 and royal icing; smooth with spatula if necessary. Attach small teardrop loops to base board with royal icing. Attach a tip 225 drop flower on top of each small loop. Pipe tip 2 dots on side of base board. **Serves 262.**＊

Gentle Curves

from page 15

from page 15

CONSTRUCTION METHOD:
Stacked, p. 56; Alternate 2-Plate Construction, p. 58

Pans:
- 8, 12, 16 x 2 in. Rounds, p. 126

Tips:
- 2, 2B, 129, 131

Ornament:
- Spring Song, p. 121

Also:
- Fluted Bowl Separator Set, p. 114
- Flower Former Set
- Cake Circles, p. 119
- Fanci-Foil Wrap, p. 119
- Plastic Dowel Rods, p. 120
- Meringue Powder
- Waxed paper
- Small plastic ruler
- Silk flowers

Cakes Needed:
- 2-layer (4 in. high) 8, 12, 16 in. Rounds

Recipes:
- Buttercream Icing††, p. 49
- Royal Icing, p. 49

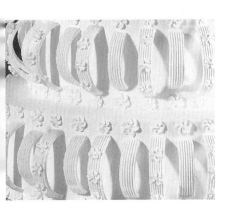

Several days in advance: Make flowers and bands using royal icing. On waxed paper, make 112 tip 131 drop flowers and 168 tip 129 drop flowers, all with tip 2 dot centers. Make extras to allow for breakage and let dry. Cover outside of medium and large flower formers with waxed paper. Make bands (p. 103).

Ice cakes smooth in buttercream and prepare for Stacked and Alternate 2-Plate Construction. Mark all cakes at top and bottom into 1¼ in. divisions. At division marks, attach alternating tip 131 and tip 129 drop flowers with buttercream. Attach bands, centered between top and bottom of cake, with buttercream; position medium bands between tip 131 drop flowers

and large bands between tip 129 drop flowers. At reception, position Fluted Bowl Separator, filled with silk flowers, on stacked cakes; position 8 in. cake on separator. Position ornament.† **Serves 156.***

*The top tier is often saved for the first anniversary. The number of servings given does not include top tier.

†Always place a separator plate or cake board, cut to fit, on the cake before you position any figurine or ornament. This protects both the cake and your keepsake. For extra stability, secure your figurine to the plate with double-stick craft tape.

††Or use Wilton Ready-To-Use Decorator Icing.

CONSTRUCTION METHOD:
Globe Pillar Set Construction, p. 59

Pans:
- 6, 10, 14 x 2 in. Rounds, p. 126
- Cookie Sheets

Tip:
- 2

Ornament:
- Elegance, p. 121

Also:
- White Ready-To-Use Rolled Fondant (150 oz.), p. 125
- Easy-Glide Fondant Smoother
- Rolling Pin
- Roll & Cut Mat
- Brush Set
- 2, 2¹/₂ in. Globe Pillar Sets, p. 115
- 3 in. Globe Base Set, p. 115
- 8, 12, 16 in. Decorator Preferred® Smooth-Edge Separator Plates, p. 117
- Paring knife
- Ruler
- Cornstarch

Cakes Needed:
- 2-layer (4 in. high) 6, 10, 14 in. Rounds

Recipes:
- Buttercream Icing††, p. 49
- Thinned Fondant Adhesive, p. 50

In advance: Make fondant balls. For consistency, roll a ¹/₄ in. log of fondant and, measuring with a ruler, cut off pieces to roll into balls, varying the length cut to the size of your ball. Roll 272 large balls, ⁷/₁₆ in. diameter, 268 medium balls, ⁵/₁₆ in. diameter, and 252 small balls, ³/₁₆ in. diameter. Let dry on cookie sheets dusted with cornstarch; set aside.

Prepare cakes for Globe Pillar Construction. Prepare for rolled fondant by lightly icing with buttercream. Cover cakes with fondant; smooth with Fondant Smoother. Attach assorted balls to cakes with fondant adhesive and tip 2.

At reception: Assemble cakes. Position ornament.† **Serves 116.***

*The top tier is often saved for the first anniversary. The number of servings given does not include the top tier.

†Always place a separator plate or cake board, cut to fit, on the cake before you position any figurine or ornament. This protects both the cake and your keepsake. For extra stability, secure your figurine to the plate with double-stick craft tape.

††Or use Wilton Ready-To-Use Decorator Icing.

Sparkling Champagne

from page 17

CONSTRUCTION METHOD:
Stacked Construction, p. 56

Pans:
- Oval Pan Set, p. 127

Tip:
- 2

Color:
- Ivory

Also:
- White Ready-To-Use Rolled Fondant (252 oz.), p. 125
- Easy-Glide Fondant Smoother
- Rolling Pin
- 6$^1/_2$ in. Cake Bow, p. 122
- Plastic Dowel Rods, p. 120
- Parchment Triangles
- Color Flow Mix
- Piping Gel
- Cake Boards, p. 119
- Fanci-Foil Wrap, p. 119
- Paring knife
- Waxed paper
- $^1/_2$ in. thick foamcore or plywood board (cut into an 18$^1/_2$ x 14$^3/_8$ in. oval)

Cakes Needed:
- 2-layer (4 in. high) 7$^3/_4$ x 5$^5/_8$, 10$^3/_4$ x 7$^7/_8$, 13$^1/_2$ x 9 $^7/_8$, 16$^1/_2$ x 12$^3/_8$ in. Ovals

Recipes:
- Buttercream Icing††, p. 49
- Color Flow Icing, p. 50

In advance: Make color flow bubbles on waxed paper-covered board. Using a cut parchment bag, make $^3/_4$ in. (100 needed), $^1/_2$ in. (125 needed), $^5/_{16}$ in. (225 needed) and $^1/_8$ in. (950 needed) diameter circles. Make extras to allow for breakage and let dry.

Prepare base board. Wrap foamcore or plywood board with foil. Lightly brush with piping gel. Tint 108 oz. of fondant ivory. Roll out fondant $^1/_4$ in. thick. Position over board using rolling pin, draping fondant over edge. Trim excess fondant from edges under bottom of board. Smooth top and sides with Fondant Smoother.

Prepare cakes for stacked construction. Prepare for rolled fondant by lightly icing with buttercream. Cover cakes with white or ivory fondant; smooth with Fondant Smoother. Position cakes. Roll white fondant balls for bottom borders: $^3/_4$ in. diameter for base cake and $^1/_2$ in. diameter for other cakes. Attach balls and color flow bubbles with tip 2 and full-strength color flow. Position bow.
Serves 141.*

Mega Mocha!

from page 18

CONSTRUCTION METHOD:
Cake Stand Construction, p. 57

Pans:
- 6, 10, 14 x 2 in. Rounds, p. 126

Tip:
- 2A

Ornament:
- Monogram Picks, p. 122

Patterns:
- Candy Frame Pieces (Small, Medium and Large), p. 104

Also:
- Round Floating Tiers Cake Stand Set (includes 8, 12, 16 in. plates), p. 118
- Flower Former Set
- Roll & Cut Mat
- Rolling Pin
- Fondant Ribbon Cutter/Embosser Set
- Light Cocoa Candy Melts®† (4 pks.)
- 8 in. Angled Spatula
- 3 in. Circle Metal Cutter
- Freezer paper
- Bamboo skewers

Cakes Needed:
- 2-layer (4 in. high) 6, 10, 14 in. Rounds

Recipes:
- Chocolate Mocha Buttercream Icing, p. 49
- Mocha Filling, p. 50
- Candy Clay, p. 51

In advance: Using 3 pks. of melted candy, make 55 candy frame pieces using large pattern and 5 each using medium and small patterns (p. 110). Reserve leftover candy.

Make 1 recipe of Candy Clay. Roll out clay 1/8 in. thick. Using small opening of tip 2A, cut 170 dots. To 28 of the large candy frame pieces and 2 each of the medium and small candy frame pieces, attach 5 dots with melted candy. Roll out remaining Candy Clay. Using zigzag-edge wheels and 1 1/4 in. spacer from Ribbon Cutter/Embosser Set, cut 33 Candy Clay strips, 4 in. long. Attach strips to remaining

27 large candy frame pieces and 3 each of the medium and small candy frame pieces with melted candy.

Dip monogram letters in melted candy and set on freezer paper to dry. Using Candy Clay, make bases for letters. Roll two 1/2 in. balls of Candy Clay each for right and left (lower) letters; flatten into 1/4 in. thick disks. Roll two 1 1/4 in. balls for center (higher) letter; flatten into 1 in. thick disks.

Fill cakes and ice smooth. Attach large candy frame pieces to sides, alternating dotted and

striped designs. Mark center of 10 and 14 in. cake tops with 3 in. metal cutter.

At reception: Position cakes on stand. Thread bases on spikes of letters, using larger bases for higher letter. Insert in cake top. Position medium and small candy frame pieces on cake tops around imprinted circles; attach seams with melted candy. **Serves 116.****

†Brand confectionery coating.

Neapolitan Charm

from page 19

CONSTRUCTION METHOD:
Globe Pillar Set Construction, p. 59

Pans:
- 6, 10, 14 x 2 in. Squares, p. 126

Colors*:
- Royal Blue, Rose, Leaf Green, Lemon Yellow

Ornament:
- Classic Couple, p. 121

Also:
- 2 in., 2¹/₂ in. Globe Pillar Sets, p. 115
- 3 in. Globe Base Set, p. 115
- 6, 10, 14 in. Decorator Preferred® Round Separator Plates, p. 117
- White Ready-To-Use Rolled Fondant (240 oz.), p. 125
- Fondant Ribbon Cutter/Embosser Set
- Brush Set
- Piping Gel
- 13 x 19 in. Cake Boards, p. 119
- Fanci-Foil Wrap, p. 119
- Crystal-Look Bowl, p. 120
- Ruler
- 7, 11, 15 in. square foamcore boards, ¹/₄ in. thick, or double-thick sturdy cardboard
- Cornstarch
- Waxed paper

Cakes Needed:
- 2-layer (4 in. high) 6, 10, 14 in. Squares

Recipe:
- Chocolate Buttercream Icing, p. 49

Several days in advance: Make fondant strips. Tint 30 oz. fondant medium rose, 36 oz. medium green and 42 oz. medium blue. Combine 8 oz. of medium rose with 32 oz. white fondant to make light rose. Combine 10 oz. medium green with 40 oz. white fondant to make light green. Combine 14 oz. medium blue with 56 oz. white fondant to make light blue. Roll out colors ¹/₈ in. thick. Using ¹/₂, ³/₄ or 1 in. spacers and cutting and embossing wheels from Ribbon Cutter/Embosser, cut assorted fondant strips; make 10 of each color using straight-edge cutting wheels and 3 of each color using zigzag or wavy-edge cutting wheels with your choice of embossing wheels. Roll out 4 oz. of white fondant ¹/₈ in. thick; cut a variety of strips with Ribbon Cutter/

Embosser. Trim all strips to 4 in. high. Let dry on cornstarch-dusted cake board.

Also in advance: Cover square base boards. Wrap boards with foil and lightly brush with piping gel. Roll out fondant ¹/₈ in. thick and cover 7 in. square in light rose, 11 in. square in light green, 15 in. square in light blue. Cover 3 in. globes with light blue fondant, 2¹/₂ in. globes with light green and 2 in. globes with light rose. Cover shorter bowl of the 2-piece Crystal-Look Bowl with light blue fondant; imprint design on sides of bowl using beaded embossing wheel from Ribbon Cutter/Embosser. Roll ³/₁₆ in. balls of light blue fondant; attach to top edge of bowl with damp brush. Let dry.

Prepare Cakes for Globe Pillar Set Construction. Ice cakes smooth in chocolate

buttercream. Position 6 in. cake on rose base, 10 in. cake on green base and 14 in. cake on blue base. Randomly attach fondant strips on cake sides leaving portions of cake exposed. Trim strips evenly at top edge of cakes. Cut out ¹/₂ in. wide fondant strips, matching colors to base board and position on top edges of cakes. Roll ¹/₂ in. matching fondant balls for each tier and attach to top edge strips with damp brush.

At reception: Assemble cakes. Position fondant-covered base and ornament on cake top. **Serves 148.****

Combine Leaf Green with a small amount of Lemon Yellow for medium green shade shown.

**The top tier is often saved for the first anniversary. The number of servings given does not include top tier.*

WILTON TIERED CAKES 77

Garden Terraces

from page 20

CONSTRUCTION METHOD:
Tailored Tiers Construction, p. 60

Pans:
- 6, 9 x 2 in. Round, p. 126
- Hexagon Pan Set (9, 12 in.), p. 127

Tips:
- 2, 3, 7, 44, 101, 352, 364

Colors*:
- Golden Yellow, Rose, Moss Green

Ornament:
- Devotion, p.121

Patterns:
- Small and Large Lattice Sections, p. 110

Also:
- Tailored Tiers Cake Display Set, p. 114
- 10 in. Plate from Crystal-Clear Cake Divider Set, p. 116
- Plastic Dowel Rods (3 pks.), p. 120
- Flower Nail No. 7
- Meringue Powder
- Cake Circles, p. 119
- Fanci-Foil Wrap, p. 119
- White Candy Melts®† (8 pks.)
- Fresh flowers
- Floral foam
- Wrapping paper, ribbon or fabric
- Craft block
- Cellophane tape or straight pins
- Waxed paper

Cakes Needed:
- 2-layer (4 in. high) 9 in. Round
- 2-layer (4 in. high) 6 in. Rounds (7 needed)

Recipes:
- Buttercream Icing††, p. 49
- Royal Icing, p. 49

In advance: Make hexagon candy plaques. Fill 12 in. and 9 in. hexagon pans 1/4 in. deep with melted candy; refrigerate until firm and unmold. Repeat for 6 additional 9 in. plaques. (You will need about 3/4 pk. Candy Melts for each 9 in. and 1 2/3 pks. for the 12 in. plaque.) Make lattice sections using patterns, tip 44 and royal icing. Make 24 small lattice sections for sides of 9 in. plaques and 6 large lattice sections for sides of 12 in. plaque. Outline sections with tip 44 bands. Make extra of each size section to allow for breakage; let dry overnight. Using royal icing, make 82 tip 101 roses with tip 7 bases and 165 tip 101 rosebuds. Make extra to allow for breakage; let dry overnight.

Ice cakes smooth in buttercream. Dowel rod all cakes to support candy plaques. Position 9 in. cake on 12 in. plate from Tailored Tiers Set and one 6 in. cake on 8 in. plate from set. Cut 6 cake circles to 7 in. diameter and wrap with foil; position six 6 in. cakes. Pipe tip 364 shell bottom border on all cakes. Add tip 3 curving vines with tip 2 tendrils and dots on cake sides. Attach 10 roses at bottom of each 6 in. cake and 12 roses at bottom of 9 in. cake; attach rosebuds to tendrils. Add tip 352 leaves. Cut a 2 x 24 in. piece of wrapping paper, ribbon or fabric for 7 1/4 in. separator and a 2 x 13 in. piece for 4 1/4 in. separator; insert into acetate wraps from separator set; follow instructions for attaching to separators (p. 60). Turn over 8 in. plate from set so that spikes are upright and position under 7 1/4 in. separator; repeat with 6 in. plate from set under 4 1/4 in. separator. Cut a craft block to approximately 7 in. diameter x 4 1/2 in. high (to match height of bottom 6 in. cakes with plaques on top). Wrap craft block with foil.

At reception: Assemble cakes. Position craft block at center, surrounded by six 6 in. cakes. Position a 9 in. plaque on each cake. Position 10 in. separator plate on foil-covered craft block, pushing feet into block so that plate rests on plaques. Position 7 1/4 in. separator, then 9 in. cake; position 12 in. plaque on 9 in. cake. Position 4 1/4 in. separator, then top 6 in. cake. Position 9 in. plaque on top cake. Using royal icing, attach small lattice sections around top 9 in. plaque and to open edges of bottom 9 in. plaques (p. 104). Attach large lattice sections to edges of 12 in. plaque. Pipe tip 3 beads on corners of all lattice pieces. Let set. Position ornament. Position fresh flowers on small pieces of foil-wrapped florist foam; position between base cakes. **Serves 104.****

*Combine Moss Green with a little Golden Yellow for green shade shown.

†Brand confectionery coating.

**The top tier is often saved for the first anniversary. The number of servings given does not include top tier.

††Or use Wilton Ready-To-Use Decorator Icing.

Roses Upon Roses

from page 22

CONSTRUCTION METHOD:
Cake Stand Construction, p. 57

Pans:
■ 8, 10, 12 x 2 in. Rounds, p. 126

Tips:
■ 2, 3, 8, 12, 124, 129, 225, 349

Colors:
■ Rose, Kelly Green

Also:
■ 3-Tier Cake and Dessert Stand, p. 118
■ Flower Nail No. 7
■ White Ready-To-Use Rolled Fondant (24 oz.), p. 125
■ Heart Cut-Outs™
■ Rolling Pin
■ Roll & Cut Mat
■ Brush Set
■ Cake Circles, p. 119
■ Plastic Dowel Rods, p. 120
■ Meringue Powder
■ 20-gauge white florist wire (45 pieces, 5 in. long)
■ 28-gauge white florist wire (26 pieces, 6 in. long)
■ White florist tape
■ Pink tulle
■ Cornstarch
■ Waxed paper
■ Cellophane tape
■ White fabric (1 1/2 yds.)

Cakes Needed:
■ 2-layer (4 in. high) 8, 10, 12 in. Rounds

Recipes:
■ Buttercream Icing††, p. 49
■ Royal Icing, p. 49

In advance: Using royal icing, prepare roses, calyxes and drop flowers, making extras of all to allow for breakage. On flower nail, make 45 tip 124 roses in light rose with tip 12 bases; let dry. On 5 in. lengths of 20-gauge florist wire, make 45 tip 8 calyxes; let dry. Attach dried roses to calyxes with royal icing; let dry. Make 400 tip 225 drop flowers in light rose and 400 in medium rose. Make 100 tip 129 drop flowers in dark rose. Add tip 2 white dot centers to all drop flowers and let dry. Using 6 in. squares of pink tulle, make at least 26 tulle puffs. Gather squares in center to form puff and attach to 6 in. lengths of 28-gauge wire with white florist tape; set aside. Make 24 fondant hearts. Roll out fondant 1/8 in. thick; cut hearts using largest Cut-Out. Let dry on board dusted with cornstarch. Using light rose royal icing and tip 8, outline and pipe in a heart at center; overpipe with a tip 3 bead heart in dark rose. Using royal icing, attach 12 tip 225 drop flowers to each fondant heart, alternating light and medium rose; add tip 349 leaves. Let dry.

Ice cake sides smooth in white buttercream; let set. Make scalloped patterns for cake sides using waxed paper. Cut 4 in. wide sheets of waxed paper long enough to wrap exactly around each cake side. Divide sheet for 8 in. cake into 6ths,

for 10 in. cake into 8ths and for 12 in. cake into 10ths. On top edge of each sheet, draw scallop pattern 1 1/2 in. deep between each division point; cut out scallops. Wrap lower portion of sheets around cake sides; secure with tape. Ice exposed areas on sides and cake top smooth with light rose buttercream. Remove sheets. Decorate each tier the same. Attach fondant hearts at each scallop point with buttercream. Attach a tip 129 dark rose drop flower at center of each scallop, followed by 2 medium rose and 1 light rose tip 225 drop flowers on each side; add tip 349 leaves. Pipe tip 8 bead bottom borders. Attach assorted drop flowers and add tip 349 leaves.

Assemble cake bouquets. For 8 in cake, tape together 10 roses with 6 tulle puffs; for 10 in. cake, tape together 14 roses with 8 tulle puffs; for 12 in. cake, tape together 20 roses with 12 tulle puffs. Cut 3 plastic dowel rods to 4 in. long; insert 1 into center of each cake. Insert bouquets into dowel rods, trim wires if needed.

At reception: Position cakes on stand. Drape fabric around stand base. **Serves 94.****

Retro Romance

from page 23

CONSTRUCTION METHOD:
Stacked Construction, p. 56

Pans:
- 6, 8, 10 x 2 in. Rounds, p. 126
- 24 Cup Mini Muffin Pan

Ornament:
- Classic Couple, p. 121

Also:
- White Ready-To-Use Rolled Fondant (120 oz.), p. 125
- Rolling Pin
- Roll & Cut Mat
- Easy-Glide Fondant Smoother
- Gum-Tex™
- Dowel Rods, p. 120
- White Sparkling Sugar (2 pks.), p. 125
- Cake Circles, p. 119
- 14 in. Silver Cake Base, p. 119, or 14 in. Cake Plate
- Piping Gel
- Cornstarch
- Paring knife
- Pastry brush

Cakes Needed:
- 2-layer (4 in. high) 6, 8, 10 in. Rounds

Recipe:
- Buttercream Icing††, p. 49

In advance: Make 20 large, 27 medium, and 23 small ribbon roses (p. 104). Knead 4 teaspoons Gum-Tex into 48 oz. of fondant. Roll out fondant 1/16 in. thick, cut 1 1/2 x 12 in. long strips for large roses and 1 x 6 in. long strips for medium and small roses. Make extras to allow for breakage and let dry in mini muffin pan dusted with cornstarch.

Prepare 2-layer cakes for Stacked Construction. Prepare cakes for rolled fondant by lightly icing with buttercream. Cover cakes with fondant; smooth with Fondant Smoother. Thin piping gel with a small amount of water and brush on cakes; immediately cover cakes with Sparkling Sugar. Assemble cakes. Attach roses to bottom borders using dots of buttercream icing, small roses on 6 in. tier, medium roses on 8 in. tier, large roses on 10 in. tier.

At reception: Position ornament.†
Serves 62.*

*The top tier is often saved for the first anniversary. The number of servings given does not include top tier.

†Always place a separator plate or cake board, cut to fit, on the cake before you position any figurine or ornament. This protects both the cake and your keepsake. For extra stability, secure your figurine to the plate with double-stick craft tape.

††Or use Wilton Ready-To-Use Decorator Icing.

Grandeur
from page 24

CONSTRUCTION METHOD:
Push-In Pillar and Stacked
Construction, p. 56, 57

Pans:
- 6, 8, 12 x 2 in. Rounds, p. 126
- 18 x 3 in. Half Round, p. 126

Tips:
- 2, 8, 16

Colors:
- Moss Green, Lemon Yellow

Patterns:
- Arch with Scrollwork, Arch Curve, p. 111

Also:
- 8, 10 in. Crystal Clear Cake Divider Set Plates, p. 116
- 9 in. Crystal-Clear Twist Legs (2 sets), p. 116
- Cake Dividing Set
- White Ready-To-Use Rolled Fondant (360 oz.), p. 125
- Pastel Yellow Ready-To-Use Rolled Fondant (48 oz.)
- Easy-Glide Fondant Smoother
- Rolling Pin
- Roll & Cut Mat
- Gum Paste Mix (5 cans)
- Wooden Dowel Rods, p. 120
- Cake Circles, p. 119
- Fanci-Foil Wrap, p. 119
- "Hidden" Pillars, p. 116
- Stepsaving Rose Bouquets Flower Cutter Set
- Confectionery Tool Set
- Fondant Shaping Foam
- Flower Former Set
- Piping Gel
- Decorator Brush Set
- Meringue Powder
- 24 x 1/2 in. thick round plywood board
- 18 x 1/2 in. thick round foamcore or ply-wood board or triple-thick cardboard
- 22-gauge cloth-covered florist wire (106 pieces, 6 in. long)
- Light green floral tape
- Cornstarch
- Waxed paper
- Toothpicks
- Scissors
- Craft block
- Craft knife

Cakes Needed:
- 2-layer (4 in. high) 6, 8, 12 in. Rounds
- 2-layer (4 in. high) 18 in. Half Rounds (bake 4 half round cakes, 2 in. high, to create a whole 18 x 4 in. round cake)

Recipes:
- Buttercream Icing††, p. 49
- Royal Icing, p. 49
- Gum Paste, p. 51
- Gum Paste Adhesive, p. 51

At least one week in advance: Make gum paste flowers, calyxes, sepals, leaves and arches. Prepare 5 batches of Gum Paste Mix. On 6 in. wires, using instructions and cutters from Stepsaving Set, make 23 buds, 39 small roses (2 rows of petals) and 14 full-bloom roses. Also using Stepsaving Set Instructions, make green calyxes, sepals, 30 leaves on wires and 60 leaves without wires. Let flowers dry completely in craft block; dry leaves on flower formers. Tape individual wires with floral tape. For arches, make 24 copies of Arch Curve pattern and tape to cookie sheets or cake boards. Cover patterns with waxed paper and dust heavily with cornstarch. Roll out gum paste 3/16 in. thick; cut out 24 arches using Arch with Scrollwork pattern with craft knife. Make extras to allow for breakage and let dry on sides to conform to Arch Curve pattern. Turn over Arch with Scrollwork pattern and trace on back to create a reverse pattern; tape reverse side down, on flat surface. Cover pattern with waxed paper and outline with lightly tinted piping gel. Carefully lay pattern, gel side down, on dried arch; lightly trace over gel lines with brush to transfer design, then lift straight up to remove pattern. Using royal icing, cover design with tip 16 bold scrolls and tip 2 thin scrolls and dots.

At least one day in advance: Prepare 24 in. plywood base board. Tint 336 oz. of white fondant light yellow and mix with 36 oz. of pastel yellow fondant; reserve 24 oz. of white fondant for drapes on cake and arches. Wrap board with foil. Brush top and sides with piping gel. Cover board with approximately 108 oz. of light yellow fondant; smooth with Fondant Smoother.

Prepare cakes for rolled fondant by lightly icing with buttercream. Position cakes on boards; place 18 in. cake on 18 in. foil-wrapped foamcore or triple-thick cardboard. Cover cakes with fondant; smooth with Fondant Smoother. Prepare 12 and 18 in. cakes for stacked construction, then place on fondant-covered board. Pipe tip 8 bead bottom borders on all tiers. Divide 18 in. cake into 12ths. Attach an arch at each division point using royal icing. Attach arches to 12 in. cake between arches on 18 in. cake. For drapes (p. 105), roll out white fondant 1/8 in. thick and cut three 3 1/2 x 2 1/2 in. strips for each arch. Pleat strips and pinch ends together. With royal icing, attach 1 strip at base of each arch and 2 more wrapping around arch to form swags; trim excess off back of swags. Roll 1/4 in. diameter fondant balls and attach to center of swags with royal icing. Cut wires from small gum paste roses and attach a 1/2 in. diameter ball of

fondant to bottom. Attach to top of each arch with royal icing; attach leaves.

Divide 6 in. cake into 6ths. Cut 4 x 4 in. fondant squares and pleat to form swags; attach at division points, 1/2 in. from top edge of cake, with royal icing. Attach 1/4 in. ball of fondant at swag points with royal icing. Divide 8 in. cake into 8ths. Cut 4 1/2 x 4 1/2 in. fondant squares and pleat to form swags. Attach and add fondant balls as with 6 in. cake.

Cut hidden pillar even with 6" cake top. Insert at center of 6 in. cake. Using florist tape, assemble a bouquet with 9 full roses, 13 rosebuds, 10 small roses and 16 leaves on wires. Insert bouquet into pillar. Assemble 2 small bouquets with remaining flowers; tape together and curl stems; position on 8 and 12 in. cakes.

At reception: push in pillars and assemble as shown. **Serves 226.***

Full-Bloom Beauty

from page 25

CONSTRUCTION METHOD:
Push-In Pillar Construction, p. 57

Pans:
- 6, 10, 14 x 2 in. Rounds, p. 126
- 18 x 3 in. Half Round, p. 126

Tip:
- 21

Also:
- White Ready-To-Use Rolled Fondant (264 oz.), p. 125
- Rolling Pin
- Roll & Cut Mat
- Easy-Glide Fondant Smoother
- 6, 10, 14, 18 in. Decorator Preferred® Smooth-Edge Separator Plates (two 18 in.), p. 117
- Cake Circles, p. 119
- 3 in. Grecian Pillars (2 pks.), p. 116
- "Hidden" Pillars (3 pks.), p. 116
- 7/8 in. wide satin ribbon (13 yds.)
- Double-stick tape
- Waxed paper
- Fresh flowers

Cakes Needed:
- 2-layer (4 in. high) 6, 10, 14 in. Rounds
- 2-layer (4 in. high) 18 in. Half Rounds (Bake 4 half round cakes, 2 in. high, to create a whole 18 x 4 in. round cake)

Recipe:
- Buttercream Icing††, p. 49

Prepare cakes for rolled fondant by icing lightly with buttercream. Cover cakes with rolled fondant; smooth with Fondant Smoother. Prepare cakes for Push-In Pillar Construction. Wrap three lengths of ribbon around each cake, overlapping ends and securing with tape. Cover cake tops with waxed paper to protect from flower stems, leaving 1 to 1½ in. of cake edge exposed, cut opening for pillar placement.

At reception: Position 18 in. cake on 18 in. plates with six 3 in. pillars. Assemble remaining cakes on same size plates using hidden pillars. For all cakes, pipe tip 21 mounds on cake tops and on 18 in. bottom plate in a circle directly below the cake above and in center of 6 in. cake. Insert fresh flower stems into mounds. **Serves 262.***

Pearl
Peaks

from page 26

CONSTRUCTION METHOD:
Stacked Construction, p. 56

Pans:
▪ 6, 8, 10, 12, 14 x 2 in. Rounds, p. 126

Tips:
▪ 1, 21, 101

Ornament:
▪ Spring Song, p. 121

Also:
▪ 16 in. Silver Cake Base, p. 119
▪ Cake Circles, p. 119
▪ Dowel Rods, p. 120
▪ Flower Nail No. 7
▪ Large (6mm) White Pearl Beading
  (3 pks.), p. 120
▪ Meringue Powder
▪ Waxed paper

Cakes Needed:
▪ 2-layer (4 in. high) 6, 8, 10, 12, 14 in.
  Rounds

Recipes:
▪ Buttercream Icing†, p. 49
▪ Royal Icing, p. 49

In advance: Using royal icing, make approximately 70 tip 101 apple blossoms with tip 1 dot centers; make extras to allow for breakage and let dry.

Ice cakes smooth in buttercream. Position 14 in. cake on base and prepare cakes for stacked construction. Pipe tip 21 shell bottom borders on all cakes. Cut pearl beads into 7 in. lengths; attach 2¼ in. apart to edges of all cakes with dots of buttercream. Attach an apple blossom at each swag point with buttercream. Position ornament.† **Serves 196.***

*The top tier is often saved for the first anniversary. The number of servings given does not include top tier.

†Always place a separator plate or cake board, cut to fit, on the cake before you position any figurine or ornament. This protects both the cake and your keepsake. For extra stability, secure your figurine to the plate with double-stick craft tape.

††Or use Wilton Ready-To-Use Decorator Icing.

Top Moment
from page 27

CONSTRUCTION METHOD:
Stacked Construction, p. 56

Pans:
- 6, 10 x 2 in. Squares, p. 126

Tips:
- 5, 19

Ornament:
- Love's Duet, p. 121

Patterns:
- Large and Small Scrolls, p. 111

Also:
- White Ready-To-Use Rolled Fondant (36 oz.), p. 125
- Easy-Glide Fondant Smoother
- Rolling Pin
- Roll & Cut Mat
- Gum-Tex™
- Meringue Powder
- Piping Gel
- Round Comfort Grip™ Cutter
- Ceramic Pedestal Cake Stand, p. 118
- 9 in. Baker's Best® Disposable Pillars with Rings (1 needed)
- Cake Boards, p. 119
- Fanci-Foil Wrap, p. 119
- Waxed paper
- 14 in. square, 1/2 in. thick foamcore or plywood board
- Cornstarch

Cakes Needed:
- 2-layer (4 in. high) 6, 10 in. Squares

Recipes:
- Buttercream Icing††, p. 49
- Royal Icing, p. 49

Several days in advance: Make 6 large and 53 small scrolls using royal icing. Place patterns on cake board and cover with waxed paper. Outline patterns with tip 19; let dry overnight. When dry, carefully lift and turn over scrolls. Overpipe on back with tip 19. Make extras to allow for breakage and let dry.

Also in advance: Prepare cake board and ornament base. For cake board, wrap 14 in. foamcore or plywood board with foil, then coat lightly with piping gel. Roll out 36 oz. of fondant; cover board with fondant and smooth with Easy-Glide Smoother. Trim off excess and let dry. For ornament base, add 1/4 teaspoon of Gum-Tex to a 2 1/2 in. ball of fondant. Roll out 3/16 in. thick; cut out circle using round cutter.

Let dry 48 hours on waxed paper-covered board dusted with cornstarch.

Ice cakes smooth in buttercream and prepare for stacked construction. Position on fondant-covered board. Pipe tip 5 bead bottom borders.

At reception: Position cake on cake stand. Insert 9 in. pillar in center of cake top. Attach 6 large scrolls to pillar with royal icing. Attach ornament base to top of pillar and scrolls with royal icing. Attach small scrolls on cake sides, 1 in. apart, with buttercream. Position ornament. **Serves 50.****

Flower Tower

from page 28

CONSTRUCTION METHOD:
2-Plate and Pillar Construction, p. 58

Pans:
8 in., 12 in., 16 x 2 in. Hearts, p. 126

Tips:
1, 2, 5, 7, 12, 101, 102, 103, 104, 352

Colors*:
Buttercup Yellow, Royal Blue, Violet, Leaf Green, Moss Green, Lemon Yellow

Ornaments:
Bianca, p. 121
Lighted Revolving Base, p. 122

Pattern:
Petal Template for 5-Petal Flower, p. 105

Also:
Cake Boards, p. 119
Fanci-Foil Wrap, p. 119
10, 14 in. Heart Separator Plates (2 each), p. 117
2¹/₂, 5 in. Curved Pillars (1 pk. each), p. 117
Dowel Rods, p. 120
Flower Nail No. 7
Lily Nail Set
Meringue Powder (8 oz. can)
Waxed paper
18 in. heart, ¹/₂ in. thick foamcore or triple-thick cardboard
Aluminum foil
Plastic wrap
¹/₂ in. wide white ribbon (4¹/₂ ft.)
Cellophane tape

Cakes Needed:
3-layer 8, 12, 16 in. Hearts (bake two 2 in. and one 1 in. high cake for each 5 in. high tier)

Recipes:
Buttercream Icing††, p. 49
Royal Icing, p. 49

Several days in advance: Make royal icing flowers. Make 325 tip 101 apple blossoms in green with tip 1 dot centers in white; 55 tip 101 full roses in light violet with tip 5 bases; 30 tip 101 medium roses (only 2 rows of petals) in light violet with tip 5 bases; 30 tip 101 5-petal flowers (p. 105) in dark violet with white tip 2 dot centers; 450 tip 102 blue/white 2-tone single petals (p. 105); 55 tip 103 full roses in dark violet with tip 12 bases; 30 tip 104 buttercup/white 2-tone roses with tip 5 bases. Make extras to allow for breakage and let dry.

Ice cakes smooth in buttercream. Prepare for 2-plate and pillar construction. Pipe tip 7 ball bottom borders. Attach flower clusters along top borders of all tiers with dots of buttercream. Add tip 352 leaves in buttercream. Pipe tip 2 dots under flower clusters on sides of cakes. Tape ribbon to sides of foil-wrapped base board.

At reception: Assemble cakes with pillars. Position revolving base and figurine.†
Serves 150.*

Combine Royal Blue with Violet for light blue shade shown on single petals and for dark blue shade shown on 5-petal flowers. Combine Violet with a little Royal Blue for light violet shade shown on tip 101 full and partial roses and for dark violet shade shown on tip 103 full roses. Combine Leaf Green with a little Moss Green and Lemon Yellow for green shade shown on apple blossoms.

**The top tier is often saved for the first anniversary. The number of servings given does not include top tier.*

†*Always place a separator plate or cake board, cut to fit, on the cake before you position any figurine or ornament. This protects both the cake and your keepsake. For extra stability, secure your figurine to the plate with double-stick craft tape.*

††*Or use Wilton Ready-To-Use Decorator Icing.*

CONSTRUCTION METHOD:
Push-In Pillar Construction, p. 57

Pans:
■ 6, 10, 14 x 2 in. Rounds, p. 126

Tips:
■ 6, 12

Colors*:
■ Lemon Yellow, Golden Yellow, Leaf Green

Also:
■ 8, 12 in. Decorator Preferred® Separator Plates, p. 117
■ 9 in. Grecian Spiked Pillars (2 pks.), p. 116
■ "Hidden" Pillars, p. 116
■ Cake Circles, p. 119
■ 16 in. Silver Cake Base, p. 119
■ White Ready-To-Use Rolled Fondant (72 oz.), p. 125
■ Neon Colors Fondant Multi Pack
■ Daisy and Leaf Cut-Outs™
■ Rolling Pin
■ Easy-Glide Fondant Smoother
■ Fondant Cutter/Embosser
■ Brush Set
■ Gum Paste Mix
■ Yellow Colored Sugar
■ White Candy Melts®†
■ 1/2 in. wide white ribbon (4 ft)
■ 18-gauge florist wire (60 pieces, 12 in. long)
■ Green florist tape
■ Ruler
■ Cornstarch
■ Wire clippers
■ Scissors
■ Waxed paper
■ Cellophane tape

Cakes Needed:
■ 2-layer (4 in. high) 6, 10, 14 in. Rounds

Recipes:
■ Buttercream Icing††, p. 49
■ Gum Paste, p. 49

In advance: Make daisies and leaves. Prepare gum paste and mix with 29 oz. of white fondant. Roll out 1/8 in. thick and cut 74 large and 114 medium daisies using Cut-Outs. Combine 3 oz. white with 1 1/2 oz. neon yellow; roll 3/8 in. balls for large and 1/4 in. balls for medium daisy centers, flatten and attach with damp brush. For leaves, tint 10 oz. fondant green. Roll out 1/8 in. thick; cut 15 medium and 56 small leaves using Cut-Outs. Let daisies and leaves dry on cornstarch-dusted surface. When dry, brush daisy centers with water and sprinkle with yellow sugar. Wrap wires with florist tape. Attach 30 large daisies, 15 medium daisies and 15 medium leaves to wires with melted candy. Let dry on waxed paper-covered cake boards.

Ice cakes smooth (sides in yellow, tops in white); prepare for Push-In Pillar Construction. For stripe colors, combine 10 oz. portions of white fondant with 4 oz. portions of neon pink, neon purple and neon orange fondant. Roll out colors 1/8 in. thick. Using straight-edge wheel from Cutter/Embosser, cut approximately 130 assorted color stripes, 1/4 in. wide. Position 1/2 in. apart on cake; trim to height of cakes. Attach large and medium daisies to top borders with tip 6 dots of icing. Pipe tip 12 ball bottom borders. Tape ribbon to sides of silver cake base.

At reception: Assemble cake. Attach medium daisies and small leaves to pillars with buttercream and tip 6. Cut a hidden pillar to 4 in. high; insert in center of 6 in. cake. Insert wired daisies and leaves in pillar. **Serves 116.**

*Combine Lemon Yellow with a small amount of Golden Yellow for yellow shade used to ice cake sides.

**The top tier is often saved for the first anniversary. The number of servings given does not include top tier.

†Brand confectionery coating.

††Or use Wilton Ready-To-Use Decorator Icing.

Exhilaration
from page 30

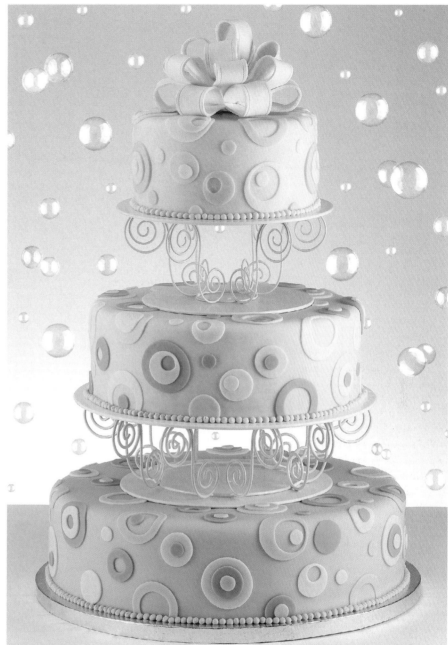

In advance: Wrap 18 in. base board with foil. Prepare cakes for Alternate 2-Plate Construction. Prepare for rolled fondant by lightly icing with buttercream.

For 16 in. cake: Tint 116 oz. fondant medium green; reserve 8 oz. for decorating. Tint 8 oz. each light and dark green. Cover cake with medium green fondant; smooth with Fondant Smoother. Roll out three shades of fondant ¹/8 in. thick; using all sizes of Cut-Outs, cut various circles. Use smaller Cut-Outs to cut portions of some larger circles. Attach to cake with damp brush, using layering and fill-in techniques described on Cut-Outs package.

For 12 in. cake: Tint 54 oz. fondant medium rose; reserve 6 oz. for decorating. Tint 6 oz.

each light and dark rose. Cover cake with medium rose fondant; smooth. Roll out three shades of rose fondant ¹/8 in. thick; cut and attach circles as for 16 in. cake.

For 8 in. cake: Tint 28 oz. fondant medium yellow; reserve 4 oz. for decorating. Tint 4 oz. each light and dark yellow. Cover cake with medium yellow fondant; smooth. Roll out three shades of fondant ¹/8 in. thick; cut and attach circles as for 16 in. cake. With buttercream, pipe tip 5 ball bottom borders on all cakes.

At reception: Assemble cake and position bow. **Serves 156.****

Pearl Necklace

from page 31

CONSTRUCTION METHOD:
Globe Pillar Set Construction, p. 59

Pans:
- 6, 10, 14 x 2 in. Rounds, p. 126

Tip:
- 3

Color:
- Rose

Pattern:
- Scallop, p. 111

Also:
- White Ready-To-Use Rolled Fondant (216 oz.), p. 125
- Rolling Pin
- Roll & Cut Mat
- Easy-Glide Fondant Smoother
- 6 1/2 in. Cake Bow, p. 122
- 8, 10, 16 in. Decorator Preferred® Smooth-Edge Separator Plates, p. 117
- 2, 2 1/2 in. Globe Pillar Sets, p. 115
- 3 in. Globe Base Set, p. 115
- Cake Dividing Set
- Cake Circles, p. 119
- 5/8 in. wide pink satin ribbon (8 ft.)
- Paring knife
- Cellophane Tape

Cakes Needed:
- 2-layer (4 in. high) 6, 10, 14 in. Rounds

Recipe:
- Buttercream Icing††, p. 49

Prepare cakes for Globe Pillar Set Construction. Prepare for rolled fondant by lightly icing with buttercream. Cover cakes with white fondant; smooth with Fondant Smoother.

For cake overlays, tint 72 oz. fondant rose. Roll out fondant 1/8 in. thick. Use Roll & Cut Mat as a guide for cutting fondant circles. For 6 in. cake, cut out a 10 in. diameter circle; for 10 in. cake, cut out a 14 in. diameter circle; for 14 in. cake, cut out an 18 in. diameter circle. Position fondant circles over cakes and smooth top; lightly smooth sides.

Divide 6 in. cake into 5ths, 10 in. cake into 8ths and 14 in. cake into eleven sections approximately 4 in. wide; mark division points 1/2 in. from top edge of cake. Mark all cakes the

same. Position scallop pattern between division points; cut out scallop, remove excess fondant.

For pearl necklaces, roll 1/4 in. diameter white fondant balls; attach on scallop edge of each tier with tip 3 dots of icing. Attach 2nd necklace 1/2 in. below. Attach 4 additional 1/4 in. fondant balls from scallop points. Attach ribbon at bottom borders with tape.

At reception: Assemble cakes. Position bow. **Serves 116*.**

*The top tier is often saved for the first anniversary. The number of servings given does not include top tier.

††Or use Wilton Ready-To-Use Decorator Icing.

A Sprinkling of Fun

from page 32

CONSTRUCTION METHOD:
Cake Stand Construction, p. 57

Pans:
- 8 x 2 in. Round, p. 126
- Standard Muffin

Tips:
- 3, 5

Colors*:
- Lemon Yellow, Rose, Violet, Kelly Green, Royal Blue

Patterns:
- Sprinkling Can, Fence Section, p. 112

Also:
- White Ready-To-Use Rolled Fondant (48 oz.), p. 125
- Flower, Leaf Cut-Outs™
- Rolling Pin
- Roll & Cut Mat
- Brush Set
- Color Flow Mix
- Gum-Tex™
- White Standard Baking Cups
- Disposable Decorating Bags
- 6 in. Lollipop Sticks
- 3-Tier Cake and Dessert Stand, p. 118
- Cornstarch
- Paring knife
- 24-gauge white cloth-covered wire (5 wires in various lengths from 10 to 12 in.)
- Waxed paper
- White fabric (1½ yds.)

Cakes Needed:
- 2-layer 8 in. Round (bake 2 layers, 1½ in. high to make a 3 in. high cake)
- 24 Standard Cupcakes

Recipes:
- Buttercream Icing††, p. 49
- Color Flow Icing, p. 50

At least 48 hours in advance: Make fondant flowers and leaves. Tint 4 oz. portions of fondant yellow, rose, green and violet with a little rose. Add ½ teaspoon of Gum-Tex to each color. Roll out ⅛ in. thick. Cut 8 flowers each in yellow, rose and violet using large Cut-Out; cut 24 green leaves using medium Cut-Out. Let all dry on waxed paper dusted with cornstarch. Make fondant sprinkling can. Add 1 teaspoon of Gum-Tex to 12 oz. of white fondant. Roll out fondant ⅛ in. thick and cut out can using pattern. Also cut one white flower using large Cut-Out. Let dry on waxed paper dusted with cornstarch. Tint portions of color flow to coordinate with flowers and leaves; also tint a portion blue. Pipe in petals and veins on leaves with cut bag. Let dry. Roll ¼ in. white fondant balls for flower centers, flatten and attach with damp brush. Make 33 fence sections: Cut ⅛ in. wide strips of white fondant and position 2 on pattern to make each section; attach at ends with damp brush. Let dry on waxed paper-covered board dusted with cornstarch. Make extras to allow for breakage. Make approximately 50 water drops on waxed paper using blue color flow in cut bag; make extras to allow for breakage and let dry. Outline sprinkling can and pipe in petals on white flower with blue color flow in cut bag; let dry. For each yellow, rose and violet flower, cut a lollipop stick to 4 in. and paint with green color flow; let dry. Attach flowers and leaves to sticks with full strength

color flow using tip 5; let dry. Attach 2 lollipop sticks to back of sprinkling can with full-strength color flow; let dry. With color flow and tip 3, attach 9-12 water drops to 5 wires in various lengths from 10 to 12 in.; let dry.

Ice cake and cupcakes smooth. Cut out additional fence sections; shape and attach around cake. Attach dried fence pieces to plates of stand with full-strength white color flow. Make 5/16 in. white fondant balls; attach to base of fences with full-strength color flow. Attach wired water drops and white flower to sprinkling can with full-strength color flow; let dry. Insert sprinkling can in cake and flowers in cupcakes. Position all cakes on stand. Drape fabric around stand base. **Cake serves 10; each cupcake serves 1.**

Combine Violet with a small amount of Rose for violet shade used.

Weather It Together

from page 34

CONSTRUCTION METHOD:
2-Plate and Pillar Construction, p. 59

Pans:
- 6, 14 x 2 in. Squares, p. 126
- Sports Ball, p. 127

Tips:
- 2, 4, 14, 18, 127

Colors:
- Rose, Leaf Green, Lemon Yellow, Royal Blue, Violet

Ornament:
- Our Day Figurine, p. 121

Also:
- 4 in. Dotted Wrapped Pillars, p. 117
- 7 in. Decorator Preferred® Square Separator Plates (2), p. 117
- Gum Paste Mix
- Wooden Dowel Rods, p. 120
- Round Cut-Outs™
- Rolling Pin
- Roll & Cut Mat
- Cake Boards, p. 119
- Silver Fanci-Foil Wrap, p. 119
- Cake Dividing Set
- 16 in. square 1/4 in. thick foamcore or double-thick cardboard
- Craft knife
- Cornstarch

Cakes Needed:
- 2-layer (4 in. high) 6, 14 in. Squares

Recipes:
- Buttercream Icing††, p. 49
- Gum Paste, p. 50

At least 48 hours in advance: Make umbrella. Prepare Gum Paste Mix following can directions; tint a 6 oz. portion rose. Roll out rose gum paste 1/8 in. thick and cut a 6 in. circle using craft knife. Center circle on Sports Ball pan half dusted with cornstarch; smooth to conform to shape of pan. Trim circle to 2 in. above bottom of pan. Divide circle in 10ths. Using large round Cut-Out, cut a scallop between each division point; points of scallop should align with division points, with scallops measuring about 3/8 in. deep. Let dry on pan. For handle, cut dowel rod to 9 in.; wrap 6 in. with rose gum paste and let dry. Attach handle to umbrella with a damp 1/2 in. ball of gum paste; let dry overnight.

Ice 2-layer square cakes smooth. Place 14 in. cake on double-thick foil-wrapped board and prepare for 2-Plate and Pillar Construction.

Pipe tip 4 bead hearts on cake sides. Pipe tip 18 shell top and bottom borders on both cakes. On 14 in. cake, overpipe bottom border with tip 127 ruffle. Edge top of ruffle with tip 14 shells. Pipe tip 4 message. On umbrella, pipe a tip 2 line from center to each scallop point. Moisten a small ball of gum paste and attach for top button.

At reception: Position 6 in. cake. Insert umbrella in cake top. Position ornament.†
Serves 75.

†*Always place a separator plate or cake board, cut to fit, on the cake before you position any figurine or ornament. This protects both the cake and your keepsake. For extra stability, secure your figurine to the plate with double-stick craft tape.*

††*Or use Wilton Ready-To-Use Decorator Icing.*

CONSTRUCTION METHOD:
Center Column Construction
(Tall Tier Stand), p. 61

Pans:
- 6, 12 x 2 in. Rounds, p. 126
- Sports Ball, p. 127

Tips:
- 2, 20, 129, 225, 349

Colors*:
- Violet, Rose, Moss Green

Patterns:
- Heart with Lovebirds, p. 113
- Top and Side Scrolls, p. 113

Also:
- Tall Tier Cake Stand Set
  (8 and 14 in. Plates, two 6¹/₂ in.
  columns, Bottom Column Bolt and
  Top Column Cap Nut Set), p. 119
- Glue-On Plate Legs (6), p. 119
- Cake Corer Tube, p. 119
- Color Flow Mix
- Meringue Powder
- 11³/₄ in. Lollipop Sticks (2 pks.)
- Cake Circles, p. 119
- Parchment Triangles
- Waxed paper
- Cellophane tape

Cakes Needed:
- ¹/₂ Sports Ball
- 1-layer (1 in. high) 6 in. Round
- 2-layer (3 in. high) 12 in. Round

Recipes:
- Buttercream Icing††, p. 49
- Royal Icing, p. 49
- Color Flow Icing, p. 50

At least 48 hours in advance: Using royal icing, make 230 tip 225 dark violet and 300 tip 129 light violet drop flowers; add tip 2 white dot centers. Make extras to allow for breakage and let dry. Using color flow, make heart with lovebirds. Prepare color flow recipe, tint ¹/₂ cup dark violet, ¹/₄ cup light violet; reserve remainder white. Tape pattern to cake board; cover with waxed paper and tape in place. Outline pattern using tip 2 and full-strength dark violet color flow; let dry a few minutes. Flow in with thinned color flow in cut parchment bag; let dry completely. Outline and flow in birds again for more definition; let dry. Using royal icing, make scrolls. Cover patterns with waxed paper; tape in place. Using tip 20, make 3 top scrolls and 40 side scrolls; make extras to allow for breakage and let dry.

Prepare cakes and cake circles for Center Column Construction. For top cake, position ¹/₂ sports ball on 6 in. round cake; ice smooth in buttercream and position on cake circle with hole cut in center to accommodate top column cap nut. Position on 8 in. plate. Use scallops on plate to divide cake, marking at every 2nd scallop. Pipe tip 20 lines from division points to top center of cake. Remove cake from plate. Ice 12 in. cake smooth and position on 14 in. plate. Pipe tip 20 shell bottom border.

At reception: Assemble Tall Tier Stand, attaching two 6¹/₂ in. columns to 14 in. plate with bottom column bolt. Position 8 in. plate over column and attach top cap nut. Position top cake on plate; pipe tip 20 zigzag bottom border, then overpipe for fullness. Insert 3 top scrolls in cake top. On 12 in. cake, attach a side scroll at each scallop of plate with buttercream.

Attach color flow heart to center column with full-strength color flow; let set, supporting with hand until secure. With buttercream, attach flowers and add tip 349 leaves around center column. Insert lollipop sticks into cake following the scallops of the 8 in. plate above. Attach top of each lollipop stick to 8 in. plate with icing. With buttercream, attach flowers and add tip 349 leaves on cake top, at bottom border of top cake and around sticks and at top border of 12 in. cake. **Serves 54.**

Combine Violet and Rose for light and dark violet shades shown.

The Perfect Favor: Make lollipops on 4 in. sticks using Wilton Wedding Shower Lollipop Mold and White Candy Melts® brand confectionery coating. Tint portion of melted candy using violet from Garden Candy Color Set. Make a tulle puff using White Tulle Circles filled with White Jordan Almonds. Tie each puff with 12 in. of ³/₁₆ in. wide lavender ribbon, inserting lollipop in each. Trim stick if needed.

CONSTRUCTION METHOD:
Stacked Construction, p. 56

Pans:
■ 6, 8, 10 x 2 in. Rounds, p. 126

Tip:
■ 12

Colors:
■ Royal Blue, Violet, Rose, Leaf Green, Golden Yellow

Also:
■ Pastel Colors Fondant Multi Pack (2 pks.)
■ Heart Cut-Outs™
■ Fondant Cutter/Embosser
■ Rolling Pin
■ Roll & Cut Mat
■ Brush Set
■ White Candy Melts®†
■ Plastic Dowel Rods, p. 120
■ Parchment Triangles
■ Cake Dividing Set
■ Ceramic Pedestal Cake Stand, p. 118
■ Cake Circles, p. 119
■ 18-gauge white cloth-covered florist wire (25 pieces, 10 in. long)
■ White floral tape
■ Waxed paper
■ Serrated knife
■ Ruler
■ Cornstarch

Cakes Needed:
■ 2-layer 6, 8, 10 in. Rounds (bake two 1½ in. layers to make 3 in. high cakes)

Recipe:
■ Buttercream Icing††, p. 49

At least 48 hours in advance: Make fondant hearts. To make lime green, combine 1 package of green with 1 package of yellow fondant. To make lavender, combine 3 oz. of blue with 3 oz. of pink fondant; add violet icing color if desired. Roll out all colors ¹/₈ in. thick; cut 5 to 7 hearts in each color using medium Cut-Out. Let dry on waxed paper covered board dusted with cornstarch. Reserve remaining fondant.

Prepare for stacked construction. Ice cakes smooth. Using cake dividing set, divide 6 in. cake into 6ths, 8 in. cake into 8ths and 10 in. cake into 10ths. Roll out fondant colors ¹/₈ in. thick. Using straight-edge wheel of Cutter/Embosser, cut 3¹/₄ x 3 in. rectangles, 5 in each color (24 total used). Cut heart shape

from center using medium Cut-Out. Attach rectangles to cake sides. Tint ¹/₂ oz. of each color of remaining fondant with coordinating icing color to darken. Roll out ¹/₈ in. thick and cut out dots with narrow end of tip 12. Attach dots to rectangles with damp brush.

Attach a cut out heart to each 10 in. wire with melted candy in cut parchment bag; let set. Using floral tape, tape wires together, bending to create a cascade effect.

At reception: Assemble cakes on stand. Cut dowel rod to 6 in. using knife. Insert in cake top; position wired hearts in dowel rod. **Serves 60.**

Perky Petals

from page 37

CONSTRUCTION METHOD:
Stacked Construction, p. 56

Pans:
- 6, 10 x 2 in. Rounds, p. 126

Tips:
- 3, 4

Colors*:
- Rose, Violet, Lemon Yellow, Kelly Green, Sky Blue

Also:
- White Ready-To-Use Rolled Fondant (72 oz.), p. 125
- Flower, Leaf Cut-Outs™
- Rolling Pin
- Roll & Cut Mat
- Fondant Cutter/Embosser
- Confectionery Tool Set
- Fondant Shaping Foam
- Brush Set
- White Candy Melts®†
- Candy Melting Plate
- Ceramic Pedestal Cake Stand, p. 118
- Cake Circles, p. 119
- Dowel Rods, p. 120
- Flower Spikes, p. 120
- Cornstarch
- Waxed Paper
- 22-gauge green cloth-covered wire (12 pieces, 9 in. long)
- Plastic ruler
- Florist tape

Cakes Needed:
- 2-layer (4 in. high) 6, 10 in. Rounds

Recipe:
- Buttercream Icing††, p. 49

In advance: Make fondant flowers and leaves. Tint 2 oz. each yellow, rose and violet. Roll out 1/8 in. thick. Cut 9 flowers in each color using large Cut-Out, 18 flowers in each color using medium Cut-Out and 9 flowers in each color using small Cut-Out. Dry all large and half of the medium flowers in each color on waxed paper dusted with cornstarch. Shape all small flowers and other half of the medium flowers using medium ball tool on thick shaping foam. Roll 1/8 in. white ball and attach to center of cupped flowers with damp brush. Dry in melting plate cavities dusted with cornstarch. Assemble 3 large and 3 small fantasy flowers in each color. For large, attach cupped medium flower to large flower with melted candy; for small, attach small flower to flat medium flower. Tint 1 oz. fondant blue and 2 oz. green. Roll out 1/8 in. thick. Cut 10 blue flowers using small Cut-Out and 15 green leaves using medium Cut-Out. Dry leaves on waxed paper dusted with cornstarch and flowers cupped same as above in curved melting plate cavities dusted with cornstarch.

Pipe tip 3 dot centers on blue flowers. For bouquet, attach 9-12 of assorted flowers to 9 in. pieces of wire with melted candy; let set.

Prepare cakes for stacked construction. Prepare for rolled fondant by lightly icing with buttercream. Cover cakes with rolled fondant; smooth with Fondant Smoother. Using wavy-edge wheel of Cutter/Embosser, score diagonal lines on each cake side, 1 1/4 in. apart. Pipe tip 3 dots at intersecting points. Pipe tip 4 bead bottom borders in buttercream. Arrange wired flowers facing forward and tape together with florist tape; trim wires as needed. Insert flower spike in center of 6 in. cake. Insert bouquet in flower spike; attach leaves to bouquet with melted candy. Attach remaining flowers and leaves to cake sides with melted candy. **Serves 40.**

*Combine Violet with a little Rose for violet shown.

†Brand confectionery coating.

††Or use Wilton Ready-To-Use Decorator Icing.

Years to Treasure

from page 38

CONSTRUCTION METHOD:
2-Plate & Pillar Construction, p. 58

Pans:
- 6, 9 x 2 in. Rounds, p. 126
- Petal Pan Set, p. 127

Tips:
- 2, 3, 18, 21, 66

Colors:
- Royal Blue, Golden Yellow

Ornament:
- Silver 25th Anniversary Pick, p. 122

Also:
- 8 in., 10 in. Decorator Preferred® Smooth-Edge Separator Plates (2 each), p. 117
- 5¹/₂ in., 2¹/₂ in. Curved Pillars, p. 117
- Lily Nail Set
- Cake Dividing Set
- Cake Circles, p. 119
- Silver Fanci-Foil Wrap, p. 119
- 1¹/₄ in. Silver Leaves
- Meringue Powder
- Plastic Dowel Rods, p. 120
- 3 in. aluminum foil squares
- 17 in. triple-thick cardboard or ¹/₂ in. thick foamcore
- ¹/₂ in. wide white ribbon (5 ft.)

Cakes Needed:
- 2-layer (4 in. high) 6, 9 in. Rounds
- 2-layer (4 in. high) 15 in. Petal

Recipes:
- Buttercream Icing††, p. 49
- Royal Icing, p. 49

In advance: Using royal icing, make 104 tip 66 bluebells in 1¹/₄ in. lily nail lined with aluminum foil. Add tip 2 dot center and pipe three tip 3 pull-out yellow stamens in each. Make extras to allow for breakage and let dry.

Ice 2-layer cakes in buttercream and prepare for 2-Plate and Pillar Construction. Position 15 in. petal cake on triple-thick cake board, cut to fit and wrapped in foil. Pipe tip 21 zigzag puff bottom border. Pipe tip 3 blue dots at each petal point. Attach 13 bluebells in rows of 4, 3, 2 and 1 on top border and down sides of each petal; attach silver leaves with tip 3 dots of icing.

Using Cake Dividing Set, divide 6 in. cake into 6ths and 9 in. cake into 8ths. At center of each division point, measure 1¹/₄ in. down from top of cake. Pipe tip 18 zigzag garland; add 4 tip 3 drop strings. Pipe tip 3 blue dots at each garland or drop string point. Pipe tip 21 shell bottom borders. Attach ribbon to edge of petal cake board.

At reception: Assemble cakes with curved pillars. Insert pick. **Serves 84.**

††*Or use Wilton Ready-To-Use Decorator Icing.*

CONSTRUCTION METHOD:
2-Plate and Pillar Construction, p. 58;
Tailored Tiers Construction, p. 60
Fountain Set-Up, p. 61

Pans:
▪ 6, 10, 14 x 2 in. Round, p. 126

Tips:
▪ 2, 3, 4, 14, 32

Ornament:
▪ Gold 50th Anniversary Pick, p. 122

Also:
▪ Kolor-Flo Fountain, p. 120
▪ Tailored Tiers Cake Display Set, p. 114
▪ 16 in. Decorator Preferred® Separator Plates (2), p. 117
▪ 13¾ in. Roman Columns (2 pks.), p. 116
▪ Cake Circles, p. 119
▪ Dowel Rods, p. 120
▪ White Ready-To-Use Rolled Fondant (144 oz.), p. 125
▪ Easy-Glide Fondant Smoother
▪ Rolling Pin
▪ Roll & Cut Mat
▪ Favorite photos

Cakes Needed:
▪ 2-layer (4 in. high) 6, 10, 14 in. Rounds

Recipe:
▪ Buttercream Icing††, p. 49

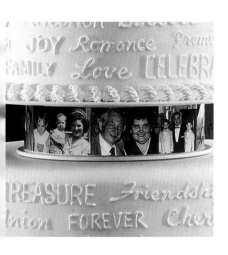

In advance: Size your photos to 2 in. high to fit in acetate holders from Tailored Tiers Set. Insert photos into acetate sleeve; follow instructions on p. 61 for attaching acetate around Tailored Tiers separators.

Prepare cakes for rolled fondant by icing lightly in buttercream. Cover cakes with fondant; smooth with Fondant Smoother. Prepare cakes for Tailored Tiers Construction and for 2-Plate and Pillar Construction.

Using tips 2, 3 and 4 and various printing styles, pipe words on cake sides in buttercream. On 14 in. cake, pipe tip 32 shell bottom border; overpipe tip 14 diagonal zigzags on each shell.

At reception: Assemble fountain. Position cakes on plates and separators. On 6 and 10 in. cakes, pipe tip 32 shell bottom borders. Overpipe shells with tip 14 diagonal zigzags as on 14 in. cake. Insert pick. **Serves 103.**

Jack Jumps for Joy!

from page 40

CONSTRUCTION METHOD:
Push-In Pillar Construction, p. 57

Pans:
- 6 x 2 in. Square, p. 126
- Petal Pan Set, p. 127

Tip:
- 2

Colors*:
- Lemon Yellow, Leaf Green, Royal Blue, Rose, Copper (skin tone)

Patterns:
- Hat, Hat Brim, Mouth p. 112

Also:
- White Ready-To-Use Rolled Fondant (48 oz.), p. 125
- Round Cut-Outs™
- Rolling Pin
- Roll & Cut Mat
- Brush Set
- Easy-Glide Fondant Smoother
- Fine Tip Neon Colors FoodWriter™ Edible Color Markers
- "Hidden" Pillars, p. 116
- Plastic and Wooden Dowel Rods, p. 120
- Comfort Grip™ Round Cutter
- 101 Cookie Cutters! Set
- Gum-Tex™
- Confectionery Tool Set
- Cake Boards, p. 119
- Silver Fanci-Foil Wrap, p. 119
- 6 in. Separator Plate, 9 in. Twist Legs from Crystal-Clear Cake Divider Set, p. 116
- 6 in. Cookie Treat Sticks
- 1/4 in. wide yellow ribbon (4 ft.)
- Ruler
- Paring knife
- Cornstarch
- Wooden skewers
- Cellophane tape

Cakes Needed:
- 2-layer (4 in. high) 6 in. Square
- 2-layer (4 in. high) 12 in. Petal

Recipes:
- Buttercream Icing††, p. 49
- Thinned Fondant Adhesive, p. 50

In advance: Make Jack-in-the-box lid and clown. After making each piece, let dry completely on cornstarch-dusted surface. Add 4 teaspoons of Gum-Tex to 48 oz. of fondant. For lid, roll out fondant 1/8 in. thick and cut into 6 in. square. Tint 4 1/2 oz. fondant rose, 4 1/2 oz. blue, 10 oz. yellow, 3 oz. green, 2 oz. copper (skin tone). For head, roll out copper fondant 1/8 in. thick and cut with round Comfort Grip cutter. Roll out white, yellow and blue fondant 1/8 in. thick; using patterns cut out mouth, hat and brim; attach. Roll and attach a 1/2 in. ball of blue fondant for pompom at point of hat. Attach brim to hat with damp brush; carefully fold pointed edges of brim forward. Roll and attach a 3/4 in. ball of rose fondant for nose. For hair, roll out rose fondant 1/16 in. thick and cut 2 x 1/8 in. wide strips. Wrap strips around skewers and let set for 10-15 minutes. Remove strips and attach to head with damp brush. When dry, draw smile and eyes with black FoodWriter. For arms, trim wooden dowel rods to 5 in. long; roll out fondant 1/4 in. thick and cut two 1 1/2 x 2 in. long strips. Wrap strips around 5 in. dowel rods, leaving approximately 3 in. uncovered; trim left arm fondant slightly shorter. For sleeve ruffles, cut two 1/2 in. wide blue fondant strips. Thin and ruffle one edge on each with ball tool from confectionery tool set; form into a circle and attach to wrists with damp brush. For collar, cut two 1 in. wide blue fondant strips; thin edge and ruffle as for sleeves to create two 1/2 circles. Attach 1/2 circles together with damp brush; let dry. For hands, shape two 1 x 7/8 in. wide pieces of green fondant; form one round end and cut notch for thumb on each. Attach to arm with damp brush. Using thinned fondant, attach cookie stick to back of head.

Also in advance: Make 4 baby bottles (p. 106).

Ice cakes smooth and prepare for Push-In Pillar Construction. Position petal cake on double-thick cake board wrapped in foil and square cake on 6 in. cake board. For block borders, roll out assorted colors of fondant 1/8 in. thick and cut into 1/2 in. wide strips, 4 and 6 in. long; attach to edges of square cake. Using letter cookie cutters, cut B, A, B, Y; attach to sides of cake. For bibs, cut assorted color fondant circles using medium round cutter from 101 Cutters Set; cut neck opening using small round Cut-Out. For scallop bib trim, cut circles using wide end of tip 2; cut in half and attach to large circle with damp brush. Print tip 2 message in buttercream. For bows, cut 1/2 x 3 in. long fondant strips; fold ends over to form bow; pinch in center to secure. For knot, cut a 1/4 x 1/2 in. fondant piece; attach and let dry. Attach bibs to cake sides with dots of buttercream. For bottom border of petal cake, roll 3/8 in. round white fondant balls; attach with dots of buttercream. Tape ribbon around base cake board.

At reception: Assemble cakes. Position 6 in. plate on twist legs. Slide baby bottles over legs and insert legs in petal cake. Attach 6 in. square cake to plate with icing. Insert clown head, position collar and insert arms in square cake. Insert an 8 in. wooden dowel rod behind clown head to support lid. Attach lid with buttercream; prop against dowel rod. **Serves 50.**

Combine Leaf Green with a little Lemon Yellow for green shade shown.

††Or use Wilton Ready-To-Use Decorator Icing.

Duck Under Cover

from page 42

CONSTRUCTION METHOD:
Alternate 2-Plate Construction, p. 58

Pans:
- 3-D Rubber Ducky, p. 127
- Sports Ball, p. 127
- Hexagon Pan Set, p. 127

Tips:
- 2, 6, 18, 32

Colors:
- Royal Blue, Golden Yellow, Lemon Yellow, Violet, Orange, Black

Also:
- Pastel Yellow Ready-To-Use Rolled Fondant
- Pastel Colors Fondant Multi Pack
- Leaf Cut-Outs™
- Gum-Tex™
- Fondant Cutter/Embosser
- Rolling Pin
- Roll & Cut Mat
- Fine Tip Neon Colors FoodWriter™ Edible Color Markers
- Meringue Powder
- White Candy Melts®†
- Rubber Ducky Candy Mold
- 4 in. Lollipop Sticks
- Duck Plastic Cookie Cutter
- Circle Metal Cookie Cutter
- 8 in. Cookie Treat Sticks
- Fluted Bowl Separator Set, p. 114
- Cake Boards, p. 119
- Fanci-Foil Wrap, p. 119
- Dowel Rods, p. 120
- Cake Dividing Set
- 6 in. Cake Circle, p. 119
- Violet curling ribbon (4 yds.)
- Craft knife
- Cornstarch
- Waxed paper
- 17 in. Hexagon double-thick card board or 1/4 in. foamcore board
- Cellophane tape

Cakes Needed:
- 3-D Rubber Ducky (use firm-textured batter such as pound cake)
- 2-layer (4 in. high) 15 in. Hexagon

Recipe:
- Buttercream Icing††, p. 49

At least 3 days in advance: Make large fondant umbrella (p. 106). Combine 1 pk. each yellow and green fondant from Multi Pack; add 1/2 teaspoon of Gum-Tex to fondant.

Also in advance: Make fondant side ducks and umbrellas. Tint 12 oz. pastel yellow fondant with Lemon Yellow color to deepen color. Roll out 1/4 in. thick. Cut 6 large ducks using plastic cutter. Let ducks dry on waxed paper-covered board dusted with cornstarch. For small ducks, dust candy mold cavities with cornstarch. Press 1/2 oz. of yellow fondant into each cavity; unmold and let dry on board dusted with cornstarch. When dry, add eyes and beak to all ducks with FoodWriter markers. Make 6 small umbrellas. For violet fondant, combine 1 oz. each pink and blue fondant and tint with Violet color. Roll out pink, blue and violet fondant 1/8 in. thick and cut circles using cutter; cut circles in half and cut scallops using wide end of tip 6. Score rib lines on umbrellas using straight-edge wheel of Cutter/Embosser. Roll small balls of fondant and attach for top button

using damp brush. Let umbrellas dry on waxed paper-covered board dusted with cornstarch. Attach lollipop stick to back of each small umbrella with melted candy.

Prepare cakes for Alternate 2-Plate construction. Position duck on 10 in. plate and ice beak smooth. Add tip 6 dot eyes. Cover body with tip 18 stars. Overpipe front wing with tip 18 pull-out stars, piped to point toward front of duck. Ice hexagon cake smooth. Attach small umbrellas to large ducks with melted candy. Roll out deep yellow fondant 1/4 in. thick; cut wings using medium Leaf Cut-Out. Attach wing to large ducks with melted candy. Attach large and small ducks, 1 in. from bottom of cake with dots of icing. Spatula stripe bag with light and dark blue icing; pipe tip 32 C-scroll bottom borders. Cut curling ribbon into five 25 in. lengths. Tape center of ribbon inside top rim of Fluted Bowl Separator.

At reception: Assemble cakes and insert large umbrella. **Serves 60.**

†Brand confectionery coating.

CONSTRUCTION METHOD:
Stacked Construction, p. 56

Pans:
- Oval Pan Set, p. 127

Colors:
- Sky Blue, Rose, Lemon Yellow, Orange, Violet, Brown, Black

Pattern:
- Ark, p. 113

Also:
- White Ready-To-Use Rolled Fondant (168 oz.), p. 125
- Gum-Tex™
- White Cake Sparkles™ (2 pks.), p. 125
- Rolling Pin
- Roll & Cut Mat
- Brush Set
- Confectionery Tool Set
- Wooden Dowel Rods, p. 120
- 6, 10 in. Cake Circles, Cake Boards, p. 119
- Fanci-Foil Wrap, p. 119
- 6 in. Cookie Treat Sticks
- 1/2 in. wide white ribbon (4 ft.)
- Craft knife
- Ruler
- Vegetable shortening
- Plastic wrap
- Cornstarch
- Scissors
- Cellophane tape

Cakes Needed:
- 1-layer (2 in. high) 10³/4 x 7⁷/8 in. Oval
- 2-layer 13¹/2 x 9⁷/8 in. Oval (bake two 1¹/2 in. layers to make 3 in. high cake)

Recipes:
- Buttercream Icing†, p. 49
- Thinned Fondant Adhesive, p. 50

Several days in advance: Make fondant animals (p. 107). For animals, tint 3 oz. each violet with a little rose, brown, yellow, orange, light rose and sky blue; also tint a 1/4 in. ball black and 2 oz. dark rose. Reserve remaining colors for rainbow.

Also in advance: Make ark, rainbow and cake top waves. For ark: Tint 12 oz. fondant light yellow; mix with 1 teaspoon Gum Tex. Roll out 1/4 in. thick. Using pattern, cut ark shape; also cut an additional hull (bottom) section. For roof sections, roll out light rose 1/8 in. thick; cut

using patterns and attach to whole ark and hull piece with adhesive. Let dry on board dusted with cornstarch. Using rolling pin, crush Cake Sparkles on waxed paper; brush roof sections with water and sprinkle with sparkles. Mark windows using pattern. Attach 1/4 in. wide dark rose strips around windows with adhesive; attach animals.

Make rainbow: For rainbow pattern, center and trace 6 in. cake circle on 10 in. cake circle. Cut out traced area. Cut remainder of 10 in. circle in half. Add 1/4 teaspoon Gum-Tex to reserved royal blue. Roll out reserved royal blue, light pink, yellow, orange and violet fondant 1/8 in. thick. Using rainbow as pattern, cut royal blue fondant base for rainbow. Cut 3/8 in. wide strips in other colors for bands of rainbow; attach over base with damp brush. Trim off any excess blue fondant and let dry on board dusted with cornstarch. With adhesive, attach sticks to rainbow, leaving 2 in. extended; attach sticks to ark, leaving 3 in. extended. Set aside.

Make free-standing cake top waves: Tape a 2 in. wide strip of waxed paper around 13¹/2 x 9⁷/8 in. oval pan; dust with cornstarch. Tint 6 oz. fondant dark sky blue; roll out 1/8 in. thick. Cut out four scalloped wave pieces, 4 to 5¹/2 in. wide and 3/4 in. deep. Let dry on side of pan, shaping around waxed paper strips to form curved shape. When dry, brush with water and sprinkle with crushed sparkles. Reserve remaining dark sky blue fondant.

Prepare cakes for stacked construction: Prepare for rolled fondant by lightly icing with

buttercream. Prepare cake board base: Tape together 4 boards and wrap with foil. Attach ribbon around sides of base with tape; position 13¹/2 in. cake. Tint 48 oz. fondant pale sky blue, 14 oz. light sky blue, 10 oz. medium sky blue. Roll out pale sky blue 1/4 in. thick, in a 20 x 16 in rectangle; cover with plastic wrap. Separately roll out light and medium sky blue, 6 oz. white and reserved dark sky blue, 1/8 in. thick, in 20 in. long pieces; cut into wavy strips from 1/4 to 1/2 in. wide. Position strips over pale blue rectangle, alternating colors; reserve any remaining strips. Using heavy pressure, roll out to blend colors together. Cover 13¹/2 in. cake with blended piece; smooth with Fondant Smoother and trim off excess. Combine excess fondant with white for a total of 24 oz. fondant. Roll out 1/4 in. thick, in a 14 x 12 in. rectangle. Position reserved strips on rectangle and repeat procedure to blend colors together. Cover 10³/4 in. cake; smooth with Fondant Smoother and trim off excess. If gaps appear between strips, blend with finger dipped in shortening. For borders, roll out reserved dark sky blue fondant 1/8 in. thick; cut 1/2 to 1 in. high wave sections, brush with water and sprinkle with crushed sparkles. Attach to bottom borders with damp brush. For clouds, roll white fondant balls 3/4 to 1 in. diameter; stack to make four 3 in. wide sections. Cover with a 1/8 in. thick layer of white fondant; trim and position on cake top. Attach free-standing waves to cake top with adhesive. Insert rainbow and ark.
Serves 40.

Teddy's Ready to Play!

from page 44

CONSTRUCTION METHOD:
2-Plate Pillar and Stacked Construction, p. 59

Pans:
- 10, 14 x 2 in. Rounds, p. 126
- Stand-Up Cuddly Bear Set, p. 127

Tips:
- 1, 2, 3, 8, 12, 16

Colors:
- Sky Blue, Rose, Lemon Yellow, Kelly Green, Black

Also:
- 11 in. Decorator Preferred® Separator Plate, p. 117
- 7 in. Grecian Spiked Pillars, p. 116
- 16 in. Silver Cake Base, p. 119
- Cake Circles, p. 119
- Fanci-Foil Wrap, p. 119
- White Ready-To-Use Rolled Fondant (48 oz.), p. 125
- Star Cut-Outs™
- Rolling Pin
- Fondant Cutter/Embosser
- Brush Set
- Gum Paste Mix (2 cans)
- Wooden Dowel Rods, p. 120
- 101 Cookie Cutters! Set
- Round Comfort Grip™ Cutter
- Cake Dividing Set
- Ruler
- Cornstarch
- Craft knife
- 5/8 in. wide ribbon (1 1/2 yds.)
- Cellophane tape

Cakes Needed:
- 2-layer (4 in. high) 10, 14 in. Rounds
- Stand-Up Cuddly Bear (use firm-textured batter such as pound cake)

Recipes:
- Buttercream Icing††, p. 49
- Thinned Fondant Adhesive, p. 50

Several days in advance: Make gum paste blocks (p. 108).

Place bear cake on foil-wrapped 6 in. cake circle. Ice paws and inside ears smooth. Cover bear except arms with tip 16 star fur. Pipe in tip 3 nose, eyes and mouth. Build up arms with tip 12; overpipe with tip 16 stars.

Ice round cakes smooth; prepare 10 in. cake for Stacked Construction. Ice sides of both cakes white, top of 10 in. yellow, top of 14 in. rose. Position 10 in. cake on separator plate. Divide 10 in. cake into 10ths, 14 in. cake into 12ths. For quilted scallops, roll out blue fondant 1/8 in. thick; cut 11 circles with Comfort Grip cutter, then cut each in half to form scallops. Using ridged wheel of Cutter/Embosser, imprint scallops with criss-cross quilt lines, 1/2 in. apart. On 10 scallops, trim 1/8 in. off each side; these will be used for the 10 in. cake. Attach scallops at division points with dots of icing. Edge scallops with tip 2 dots. Pipe tip 1 dots where quilt lines meet. Roll out rose, green, yellow and blue fondant 1/8 in. thick; cut a variety of stars using small and medium Cut-Outs. Attach stars to cake sides with icing. Pipe tip 8 ball bottom

borders. For buttons, roll 22 white fondant balls, 1/2 in. diameter; flatten to a 1 in. circle. Indent center of circles with flat end of craft knife. Use small opening of tip 1 to punch 2 holes in each button; attach at scallop points with icing.

Attach ribbon around sides of silver base with tape; position 14 in. cake on base. Insert pillars into 14 in. cake; position blocks over pillars then position 10 in. cake and bear. **Serves 103.**

††Or use Wilton Ready-To-Use Decorator Icing.

The perfect favor: Create the cutest candy bags using Wilton Favor Accents like bears, rocking horses, safety pins and newborn babies (p. 127). Make a tulle puff using White Tulle Circles (p. 126) filled with Pillow Mints (p. 127): Place mints in center of tulle circle, gather ends and tie with 6 in. of 1/4 in. wide curling ribbon. Attach favor accent with hot glue gun.

Great Anticipation

from page 46

CONSTRUCTION METHOD:
2-Plate and Pillar Construction, p. 58

Pans:
- 8 x 2 in. Round, p. 126
- Petal Pan Set, p. 127

Tips:
- 3, 8, 12

Also:
- 10 in. Decorator Preferred® Smooth-Edge Separator Plates (2), p. 117
- Embroidered Wrapped Pillars, p. 117
- Easter Eggs Candy Mold Set
- White Ready-To-Use Rolled Fondant (144 oz.), p. 125
- Gum Paste Mix
- Round, Flower Cut-Outs™
- 11 3/4 in. Lollipop Sticks
- Confectionery Tool Set
- Fondant Shaping Foam
- Easy-Glide Fondant Smoother
- Brush Set
- Meringue Powder
- Wooden Dowel Rods, p. 120
- Fanci-Foil Wrap, p. 119
- 5/8 in. wide white satin ribbon (28 in.)
- Heavy-duty board (plywood, foamcore or triple-thick cardboard)
- Cornstarch

Cakes Needed:
- 2-layer (4 in. high) 8 in. Round
- 2-layer (4 in. high) 15 in. Petal

Recipes:
- Buttercream Icing††, p. 49
- Royal Icing, p. 49

At least 4 days in advance: Make carriage, wheels and carriage trims (p. 108). Prepare gum paste and mix with 24 oz. fondant. This mixture will be used for carriage, wheels and cake flowers. Trim 4 lollipop sticks to 9 3/4 in. long. Dampen end of sticks; wrap a 1/2 in. fondant/gum paste ball over end and flatten top to create a support base for carriage; let dry.

Also in advance: Make flowers. Roll out fondant/gum paste mixture 1/8 in. thick. Cut 150 flowers using smallest flower Cut-Out. Place flowers on fondant shaping foam and

cup using small ball tool. Let flowers dry on board dusted with cornstarch; add tip 3 dot centers in royal icing.

Prepare cakes for 2-Plate and Pillar Construction; prepare cakes for rolled fondant by lightly icing with buttercream. Cover cakes with fondant; smooth with Fondant Smoother. Position 8 in. round cake on 10 in. separator plate and 15 in. petal cake on heavy-duty board cut to fit and wrapped with foil. Attach flowers to bottom border of round cake with dots of royal icing. Tie ribbon around cake. On petal cake, pipe tip 12 bead bottom border. Divide each petal section in 3rds. In buttercream, pipe tip 3 double and triple drop strings at division points. Bottom of triple drop string is 2 in. from top edge of cake; bottom of double drop string is 1 1/2 in. from top edge of cake. Pipe tip 8 balls at top drop string points. To make ruffles for petal cake, roll

fondant/gum paste mixture 1/16 in. thick. For each petal section, cut strip 1 1/2 x 12 in. long. Gather at top to make ruffle (p. 102) and individually attach to each petal with damp brush. For draped effect, position sides of ruffles 1 1/2 in. from cake bottom in corners of each petal and center of ruffles 1 in. from bottom. With royal icing and tip 3, attach flowers to top edge of ruffles and add dots on ruffles.

At reception: Position 8 in. cake on pillars. Insert lollipop sticks in top of cake and position carriage on supports, securing with royal icing. Attach wheels with dots of royal icing.
Serves 68.

CONSTRUCTION METHOD:
2-Plate Pillar and Stacked
Construction, p. 59

Pans:
- 6, 8 x 2 in. Rounds, p. 126
- 12 x 18 x 2 in. Sheet, p. 126

Tips:
- 2, 3, 5, 16, 17, 19, 129, 225, 349

Colors:
- Rose, Moss Green

Ornament:
- Inspirational Cross, p. 122

Also:
- 3 in. Curved Pillars, p. 117
- 10 in. Decorator Preferred® Smooth-Edge Separator Plates (2), p. 117
- Cake Boards, p. 119
- Fanci-Foil Wrap, p. 119
- Wooden Dowel Rods, p. 120
- Garland Marker
- Meringue Powder
- Waxed paper
- 1/2 in. wide white ribbon (65 in.)

Cakes Needed:
- 2-layer 6, 8 in. Rounds (bake 2 layers, 1 1/2 in. high to make 3 in. high cakes)
- 2-layer (4 in. high) 12 x 18 in. Sheet

Recipes:
- Buttercream Icing††, p. 49
- Royal Icing, p. 49

In advance: Make flowers using royal icing. Make 115 tip 129 drop flowers in light rose with tip 3 white dot centers. Make 155 tip 225 drop flowers in light rose and 225 tip 225 drop flowers in dark rose, all with tip 2 white dot centers. Make extras of all to allow for breakage and let dry on waxed paper-covered boards.

Ice cakes smooth in buttercream and prepare for Pillar and Stacked Construction. On sheet cake, mark sides for garlands 3 in. apart and 2 to 2 1/2 in. from base of cake. Pipe tip 19 shell bottom border. Pipe tip 17 zigzag garland starting at 2 in. high mark, to base of cake. Attach assorted drop flowers to garland; add tip 349 leaves. Starting from 2 1/2 in. mark, pipe tip 3 double drop strings, 1 1/4 in. from base of cake at deepest point. Add tip 3 dot at string

points. Pipe tip 17 shell top border. Add tip 5 message. On 6 in. cake, pipe tip 16 shell bottom border; on 8 in. cake, pipe tip 19 shell bottom border. Mark sides for garlands 2 in. apart. Pipe tip 3 double drop strings from top edge of cakes, 1 1/4 and 1 1/2 in. deep. Pipe tip 17 band on top edge of cakes. Attach assorted drop flowers to band, alternating large and small. Add tip 349 leaves. Position ornament.†
Serves 104.

†*Always place a separator plate or cake board, cut to fit, on the cake before you position any figurine or ornament. This protects both the cake and your keepsake. For extra stability, secure your figurine to the plate with double-stick craft tape.*

††*Or use Wilton Ready-To-Use Decorator Icing.*

Special Techniques

Follow these step-by-step instructions to duplicate the special decorations featured on tiered cakes in this book. You'll find flowers, borders, cake top accents and more. For a complete decorating guide, including techniques for flowers and borders not shown here, see any annual edition of The Wilton Yearbook of Cake Decorating or visit our website at www.wilton.com

Ruffles

(See Color Harmony, p. 65, Weather It Together, p. 90 or Great Anticipation, p. 100.)

A ruffle can be gently flowing or tightly gathered as shown here. To create a softer looking ruffle, after cutting your fondant section, roll the ball tool, dipped in cornstarch, along one edge.

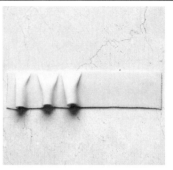
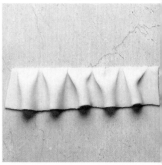

1. Roll out fondant ⅛ in. thick on your Roll & Cut Mat lightly dusted with cornstarch. Cut a strip following size stated in cake directions. As a general rule, you will need enough strips to total 2 to 3 times the length of the size you will need for the finished ruffle.

2. Starting on left side, fold small sections of the strip together vertically to form individual ruffles. As a section is done, continue adding strips by tucking cut end under the previous ruffle. Continue forming ruffles to complete desired length.

3. Attach ruffle to cake as stated in cake directions.

Bows

(See A Rainbow of Romance, p. 65 and Sparkling Champagne, p. 75.)

Nothing says "celebrate" like a cake topped with a lush fondant bow. While the bow looks intricate, it's really just a grouping of fondant strips, folded, wrapped and arranged to create a full effect. When you cut strips with the Fondant Ribbon Cutter/Embosser, you can create bows with stripes or beaded edge embossed designs.

For a time-saving alternative to fondant bows, use the pre-made Wilton 6½ in. Cake Bow (p. 122). Hand-made of paper clay, it has a beautiful full shape and can be easily tinted with icing color or non-toxic chalk to complement any setting.

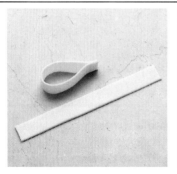

1. This bow can be assembled directly on the cake or ahead of time, using a 2 to 2½ in. fondant circle as a base. Cut strips for bow loops using dimensions listed in project instructions. Your bow may use more loops than shown here. Fold strips over to form loops. Brush ends lightly with damp brush. Align ends and pinch slightly to secure. Stand loops on side to dry.

2. Position 6 or 7 bow loops in a circle to form base of the bow. Attach to fondant circle with thinned fondant adhesive or melted candy.

3. Attach remaining loops, filling in center area of bow. Trim loop ends, if needed, to fit.

Wired Gum Paste Flowers

(See Petal Poetry, p. 68.)

The same cupped blossoms used in the cake top bouquet may also be used without wires as part of the cake side vines. If your design calls for individual wired flowers, remember never to insert the wire directly into the cake; instead, insert Wilton Flower Spikes in the cake to hold the wires.

1. Roll out rose gum paste mixture 1/16 in. thick and cut 60 flowers using pansy cutter from Floral Collection Kit.

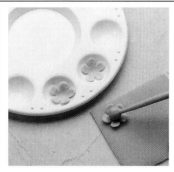

2. Place on thick foam and cup petals with ball tool from Confectionery Tool Set; let dry in small flower former or candy melting plate dusted with cornstarch. Add tip 3 dot center using royal icing.

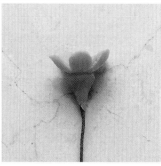

3. Make 60 stems using 22-gauge wires. Make a small hook on one end of each wire. Roll a ball of green gum paste the size of a small pea. Dip hook in gum paste adhesive, then thread ball on wire until hook is buried. Attach flowers with royal icing. Follow instructions on p. 68 for making bouquet.

Gum Paste Flowers

(See Stucco Trio, p. 71.)

The heart-shaped petals of these fantasy flowers can be made with any size heart cutter. For a smaller flower, use the smallest cutter from our Nesting Hearts Cutter Set.

1. Prepare 1 can gum paste; tint red. Roll out 1/16 in. thick. For each large flower, cut 5 hearts using largest Cut-Out; for each medium flower cut 5 hearts using medium Cut-Out. Place each heart on thin foam and ruffle top edge with ball tool.

2. Attach 5 hearts together in overlapping fashion, brushing overlapping areas with gum paste adhesive. Let large flowers dry in mini ball pan cavities dusted with cornstarch; use mini muffin cavities to dry medium flowers. When dry, brush flowers with non-toxic purple chalk which has been grated in tea strainer.

3. To make fantasy flowers, attach medium flowers inside large flowers using adhesive. Using royal icing, pipe tip 3 stamens in all flowers; let dry.

Icing Bands

(See Gentle Curves, p. 73.)

Alter the look of these pretty royal icing bands by piping with tip 2B smooth side up. You can also substitute other decorations for the flowers on top—shells, beads, or zigzags would work beautifully.

1. Cover outside of medium and large flower formers with waxed paper. Using tip 2B (serrated side up) and royal icing, make 56 bands each on medium and large flower formers. Make extras to allow for breakage and let dry.

2. While large bands are drying, attach 3 tip 129 drop flowers with royal icing; let dry.

3. Attach alternating large and medium bands to cake following instructions on p. 73.

Candy Frame Pieces

(See Mega Mocha, p. 76.)

Try to avoid handling the candy pieces with your bare hands. Fingerprints will mar the smooth, shiny appearance of the candy and the warmth of your hands can easily cause melting. Whenever picking up candy, wear cotton gloves.

1. Trace Candy Frame Piece Patterns (p. 110) on freezer paper; (see p. 76 for quantities and sizes needed). Cut out with scissors and place shiny side up on flat surface. Place 1 wooden skewer on each side of pattern as a guide for spreading candy 1/8 in. thick edge to edge. Using angled spatula, spread melted candy evenly over pattern. Lift pattern, clean edges with fingertips. Let set for 30-60 seconds until it starts to lose its wet, shiny appearance.

2. Place covered patterns on medium flower formers; refrigerate until firm. (Make extras to allow for breakage.) Peel freezer paper from candy pieces; set aside. Cut and attach Candy Clay decorations following instructions on p. 76.

3. At reception, position pieces on cake following instructions on page 76.

Lattice Section Assembly

(See Garden Terraces, p. 78.)

If you need to serve a larger cake with a larger hexagon candy plaque, you may adjust the lattice pattern size. Don't enlarge pattern with a copier—that will also enlarge the depth. instead, make a duplicate copy of the pattern, cut out the extra width you need, and attach to the original pattern.

1. Position hexagon candy plaque on cake. Attach one lattice section to an open edge of plaque with royal icing.

2. Attach another lattice section next to the first. Fill in any gap between sections with tip 3 and royal icing. Continue attaching sections to all open edges of plaques.

3. Pipe tip 3 beads on corners of all lattice pieces. Let set.

Ribbon Roses

(See Retro Romance, p. 80.)

These elegant fondant roses can be rolled tighter or fuller as you wish. For a more casual look, with a graceful rolled edge, double the width of your fondant strip, then fold in 1/2 and begin rolling.

1. Cut fondant strips following dimensions stated.

2. Begin rolling fondant strips lightly from one end, gradually loosening as flower gets larger. Roll large roses 2 1/4 in. diameter, medium 1 1/4 in. diameter, and small 1 in. diameter. Pinch bottom to gather and secure.

3. Trim flower bottom to desired height with scissors. Dust mini muffin pan cavities with cornstarch and set roses in cavities to dry.

Fondant Draping

(See Grandeur, p. 81.)

The luxurious folds of a fondant drape add richness as a side garland or as skirt accents. Make a larger, more dramatic drape by cutting a larger rectangle. Be sure not to roll out fondant too thick before gathering—the weight of the drape may tear the ends.

1. Roll out fondant ⅛ in. thick on Roll & Cut Mat lightly dusted with cornstarch. Cut rectangles in sizes and number stated in cake instructions.

2. Immediately gather the short ends and pinch together to form drapes. Trim ends with scissors to taper if needed.

3. Attach drapes to cake by brushing back with water.

Single Petals

(See Flower Tower, p. 85.)

Use these pretty royal icing petals to fill in areas on your bouquets and vines. They also make great cake top accents on garden-themed designs.

1. Attach 1½ in. waxed paper square to flower nail. Using tip 102 and royal icing in a spatula striped bag, pipe petal: squeeze bag, turn nail as you move tip ⅜ in. out from center and back. Relax pressure and return to center.

2. Repeat 3 to 4 times on each square, making sure that petals do not touch. Remove waxed paper square from flower nail; let petals dry on cake board.

3. Pipe icing on cake where petals will be positioned. Add petals and fill in as needed.

5-Petal Flower

(See Flower Tower, p. 85)

These delicate blossoms are made on a plastic wrap-covered flower nail. The plastic wrap conforms to the shape of petals better than waxed paper and makes it easy to lift flowers for placement inside a foil cup for drying.

1. Make a foil cup to dry each flower: Press a 3 x 3 in. foil square about ½ depth into lily nail, remove. Repeat to make 30 foil cups.

Attach petal template onto flower nail, cover with 1½ in. square of plastic wrap. Using tip 101 and royal icing, pipe an elongated petal following division mark on template. Squeeze bag, turn nail as you move tip ½ in. out from center and back. Relax pressure as you return to center. Repeat for 4 more petals.

2. Position flower on plastic wrap in foil cup and let dry.

3. Pipe tip 2 dot royal icing center on each flower.

Fondant Leaves

(See Love Tops The Tiers, p. 67; Perky Petals, p. 93; Stucco Trio, p. 71.)

To create a variety of curved shapes, use both sides of Flower Formers to dry leaves. You can also add a colorful flair to leaves by brushing them with a mix of clear vanilla and icing color.

1. Roll out fondant 1/8 in. thick on Roll & Cut Mat lightly dusted with cornstarch. Cut leaves using Cut-Outs™, cookie cutters or cutters from one of our gum paste decorating sets such as the Stepsaving Rose Bouquets Flower Cutter Set.

2. For veined leaves, place leaf on thin foam. Using veining tool, mark vein lines, starting with center line. Add branch veins on both sides of center line.

3. Remove leaf from foam and let dry. For curved leaves, dry on flower formers dusted with cornstarch.

Baby Bottles

(See Jack Jumps for Joy!, p. 96.)

After you've wrapped the hidden pillar with fondant, be sure to immediately "shave" into hexagonal sides. The fondant must be cut when soft to create a smooth shape. After shaving, use an Easy-Glide Fondant Smoother to sharpen the corners on each side.

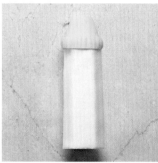

1. Cut 4 hidden pillars to 4 in. lengths. Roll out white fondant 1/4 in. thick and attach to pillars with damp brush; trim off excess.

2. To create hexagon bottle shape, using a paring knife, pare fondant on pillar from top to bottom forming 6 equal sides. Trim off 1/4 in. of fondant from top of bottle, leaving hidden pillar extended. Smooth with Fondant Smoother.

3. For bottle caps, shape a 1 1/2 x 1 1/2 in. dome of yellow fondant; cut out center with plastic dowel rod and attach at top of

bottle with thinned fondant adhesive. Insert a 6 in. plastic dowel rod into each bottle; pinch top of cap around dowel rod to form a point. For seam on bottle caps, cut 1/2 in. wide yellow fondant strips; score notches on sides with paring knife; attach to bottom edges of caps with damp brush. Remove dowel rod before drying.

Large Fondant or Gum Paste Umbrella

(See Duck Under Cover, p. 97; Weather It Together, p. 90.)

Make this enchanting cake topper several days in advance to allow sufficient drying time on the Ball Pan. You may use a Fondant/Gum Paste mixture or Gum Paste alone.

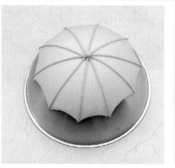

1. Roll out fondant/gum paste 1/8 in. thick and cut a 6 in. circle with knife, using a cake circle as pattern. Generously dust the outside of one ball pan half with cornstarch and position circle on top. While still on pan, using Cake Dividing Set, divide circle into 10ths. Using circle cutter for Duck Under Cover cake or large round Cut-Out for Weather It Together cake, cut a scallop between each division, approximately 3/8 in. deep. Let dry on pan for 3 days.

2. Pipe tip 2 rib lines in royal icing from top center of umbrella down to each scallop point. Roll a small fondant ball for button and attach with damp brush.

3. Remove from pan. For Duck Under Cover cake, attach cookie treat stick handle with melted candy; let set. For Weather It Together cake, cut a wooden dowel rod to 9 in. for handle, wrap 6 in. with rose gum paste and let dry. Attach handle to umbrella with a damp 1/2 in. ball of gum paste. Let dry overnight.

Fondant Animals

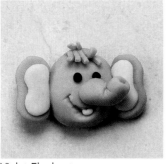

(See The Ark Arrives, p. 98.)

Each of these adorable animals is made using the same basic shapes. Follow the instructions to create ball heads, log necks, teardrop ears, ball eyes and noses, cone beaks and more. Attach all pieces with a damp brush. It's an easy way to add character to shower and birthday cakes.

Violet Elephant
Make a 1 1/8 in. flat ball head. Use knife to score a smile line; widen with veining tool from set. For eyes, roll 1/8 in. black balls. Make 1/2 in. ball ears; flatten, shape and indent center with small end of ball tool. Add a small amount of rose for tongue and inside ears. For trunk, shape a 1/2 in. ball into a log; shape and open end with small end of ball tool. For hair, roll out violet fondant and cut slits with scissors.

Brown Bear
Make a 1 in. ball head and a 1/2 in. ball snout. Add smile line. Make tongue, nose and eyes as for elephant. Make 1/4 in. flat ball ears; cut rose circles for inside ears. Make hair as for elephant. Make 1/2 in. ball paws; indent center with lollipop stick. Score claws with knife.

Yellow Giraffe
Make 2 x 1/2 in. log neck and 1 x 1 1/4 in. log head; make a 1 3/4 x 1/2 in. flat ball for snout. Add smile line and indent nostrils with veining tool. Add eyes as for elephant. Make 1/4 in. orange log horns; add 1/8 in. ball tips. Make 1/8 in. flat orange balls for spots. For ears, make 1/4 in. flat balls and shape into triangles; add a small amount of rose for tongue and inside ears.

Pink and Blue Bunnies
Make 1 in. ball head in light pink or blue. Add smile line and make eyes as for elephant. Make 5/8 x 1/4 in. teardrop shaped ears; add small amount of white inside ears. Roll small white ball teeth and dark pink nose.

Bluebird
Shape a 3/8 in. ball of dark blue in a teardrop for body; add 1/4 in. ball head. Add ball eye. Cut and flatten small pieces for wings and a small orange cone for beak.

Yellow Ducks
Make bodies and heads on a waxed paper-covered board before decorating cake. Attach to cake and add facial features after attaching waves to cake. Roll 3/4 in. oval bodies and 1/2 in. ball heads; attach to cake with icing. Shape and attach orange cone beak and 1/8 in. black ball eyes with damp brush.

Baby Blocks

(See Teddy's Ready to Play!, p. 99.)

Hollow blocks, constructed of 4 gum paste squares, are a fun way to camouflage pillars between tiers—the pillars bear the weight. The fondant lettering which decorates each block can be accented with other cut fondant shapes such as hearts or stars using small Wilton Cut-Outs.

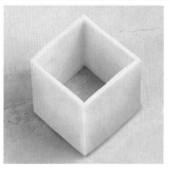

1. Prepare 2 cans of gum paste. Roll out 1/8 in. thick; cut 16 squares, 3 x 3 in. Let dry overnight on cornstarch-dusted boards. The next day, turn squares over and let dry completely overnight. When dry, attach squares side-to-side with thinned fondant adhesive to form blocks; let dry.

2. Add trims. Tint 24 oz. of fondant blue and 6 oz. each in light rose, green and yellow; reserve remaining white fondant.

   Using alphabet cutters from 101 Cookie Cutters Set, cut 4 green B, 4 yellow A, 4 rose B and 4 blue Y letters. As needed, cut out centers of letters with craft knife. Attach letters to blocks with damp brush. For borders, cut assorted fondant strips, 1/4 x 3 in. long; attach with damp brush. Let dry.

3. At reception, completed blocks will be positioned around pillars on 14 in. cake. The 10 in. cake and the bear cake will be placed on top.

Carriage, Wheels and Trims

(See Great Anticipation, p. 100.)

This carriage stands on lollipop stick legs, which are attached to the bottom with balls of fondant. After rolling the fondant balls, be sure to press them lightly against the bottom of the egg mold so that they will conform to its shape without gaps.

1. For carriage bottom, dust outside of rounded half (no flat bottom) of largest mold from Easter Eggs Mold Set. Roll out fondant/gum paste mixture 1/16 in. thick and position on egg mold half; trim off excess even with bottom of mold; let dry completely on mold for 1 to 2 days. For carriage hood, repeat process used for carriage bottom. Trim off 2 1/2 in. from larger end of egg; let dry 1 to 2 days.

2. To assemble carriage, attach hood to bottom with tip 3 and royal icing. Pipe tip 3 beads around seam.

3. For wheels, roll out fondant/gum paste mixture 1/8 in. thick. Cut 4 wheels with largest round Cut-Out. For carriage trims, roll out fondant/gum paste mixture 1/16 in. thick. Cut 20 circles using smallest round Cut-Out; cut circles in half. Let wheels and trims dry on board dusted with cornstarch.

Set aside. Attach half-circle trims to rim of carriage hood and bottom with royal icing. Pipe tip 3 spirals on wheels. Attach wheels to lollipop sticks and position carriage at party.

Note: *For flowers, other techniques and products not shown in this book, see "The Wilton Yearbook of Cake Decorating" or visit www.wilton.com.*

Patterns

Using Patterns

In order to reproduce our cake designs exactly as shown in this book, patterns must be followed for certain decorations. If you will be using different cake sizes than those stated in instructions, you will need to adjust patterns accordingly. Use a copier to make patterns larger or smaller, based on the percentage of size difference in your cake. Wilton grants permission to copy all patterns in this book.

How To Transfer Patterns Using Piping Gel

1. Make copy of pattern. Turn copy over and trace pattern on back to create a reverse pattern. Tape pattern, reverse side down, on flat surface.
2. Cover pattern with waxed paper and outline with piping gel.
3. Carefully lay outlined pattern, gel side down, on iced cake that has crusted. Using a Decorator Brush, gently trace over gel lines. To remove, lift pattern straight up from cake.

Using a Toothpick

1. Tape pattern to flat surface, such as back of cake circle, cookie sheet or counter top. Cover with waxed paper and smooth out all wrinkles. Trace pattern onto the waxed paper with a Wilton FoodWriter™ Edible Color Marker.
2. Ice cake and let icing set until it has a slight crust. Position waxed paper pattern gently on top or side of cake and secure very lightly with sharp toothpicks.
3. Using toothpick, carefully imprint along pattern lines to transfer a dotted line of pattern onto cake.
4. Remove toothpicks and waxed paper pattern. Connect dots with icing outlines. Cover the shape with decorations needed.

Scrolls & Hearts (see "Brilliant Future", p. 66)

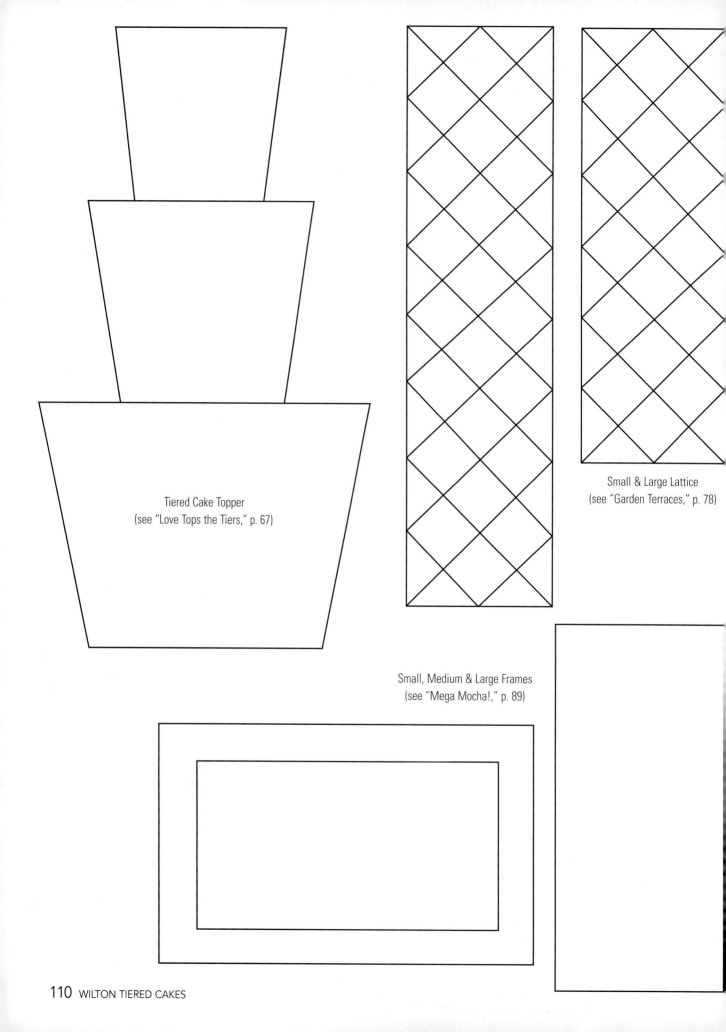

Tiered Cake Topper
(see "Love Tops the Tiers," p. 67)

Small & Large Lattice
(see "Garden Terraces," p. 78)

Small, Medium & Large Frames
(see "Mega Mocha!," p. 89)

Arch with Scrollwork
(see "Grandeur," p. 81)

Small & Large Teardrop Loops
(see "Love's Legacy," p. 72)

Large

Small

Arch Curve
(see "Grandeur," p. 81)

Scallop
(see "Pearl Necklace," p. 88)

Small Scroll

Petal Template
(see "Flower Tower," p. 85)

Large & Small Scrolls
(see "Top Moment," p. 84)

Large Scroll

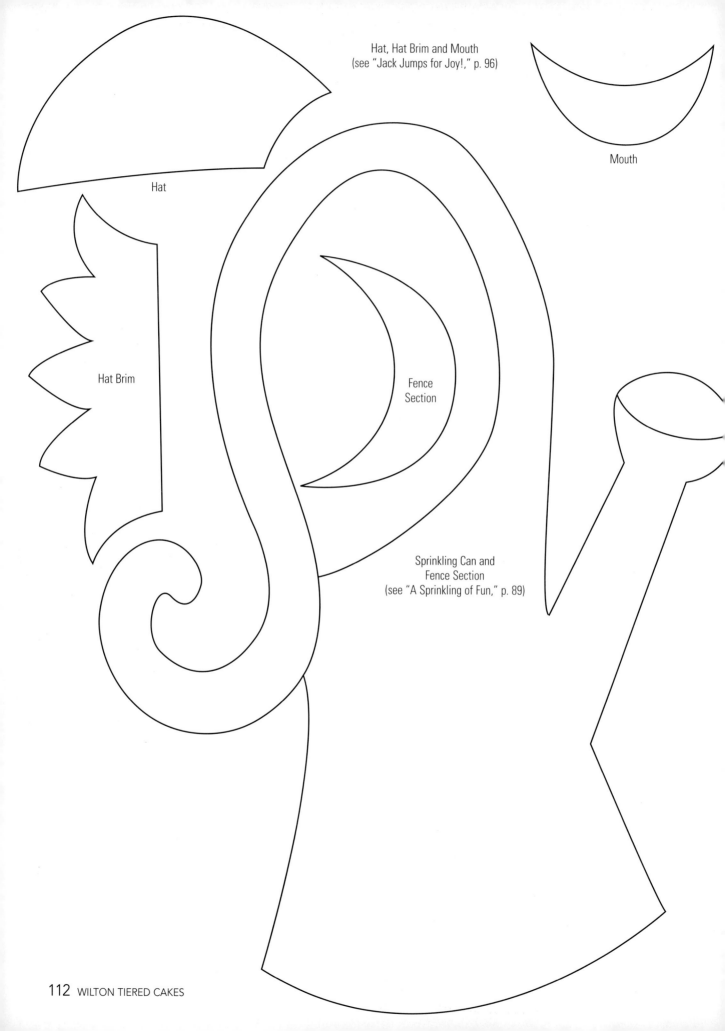

Hat, Hat Brim and Mouth
(see "Jack Jumps for Joy!," p. 96)

Mouth

Hat

Hat Brim

Fence
Section

Sprinkling Can and
Fence Section
(see "A Sprinkling of Fun," p. 89)

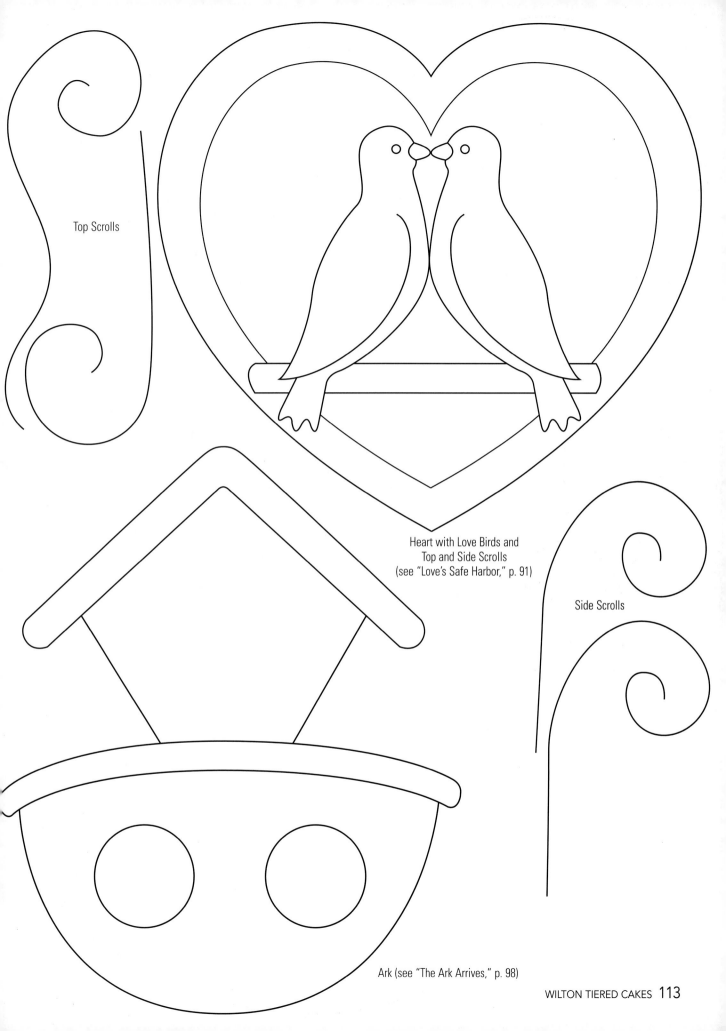

Top Scrolls

Heart with Love Birds and
Top and Side Scrolls
(see "Love's Safe Harbor," p. 91)

Side Scrolls

Ark (see "The Ark Arrives," p. 98)

Tiered Cake Products

Wilton products help you present the most exciting tiered cakes in the world. From cake stands and separators to ornaments and accents, Wilton products enhance our cake designs so that you can create a distinctive look perfect for your big event. Here is just a sample of Wilton essentials for baking, decorating and assembling cakes in this book. For a complete product selection, see the annual edition of the "Wilton Yearbook of Cake Decorating" or visit our website, www.wilton.com.

Cake Assembly Sets

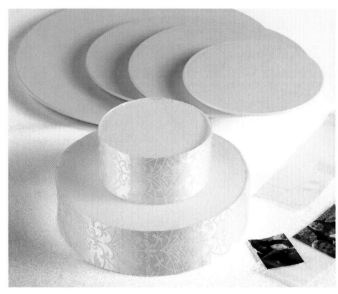

Tailored Tiers Cake Display Set

Satin-look separators add beautiful texture to any tiered cake design. The elegant patterned fabric which covers the foam separators will complement most wedding, shower and anniversary designs and looks wonderful with floral arrangements. As an added bonus, use the included acetate photo wraps to customize the separators with treasured family photos, wrapping paper or an alternate fabric. It's a great way to personalize your cake for those special occasions.

Set includes 2 satin brocade wrapped craft foam separators ($4^{1}/_{4}$ and $7^{1}/_{4}$ in. diameter x 2 in. high), 4 smooth-edge separator plates (one 6 in., two 8 in., one 12 in. diameter) and 2 acetate photo wraps. The $4^{1}/_{4}$ in. separator holds cakes up to 6 in. diameter when used with 8 in. top plate; the $7^{1}/_{4}$ in. separator holds cakes up to 10 in. diameter when used with 12 in. top plate.
304-8174

Fluted Bowl Separator Set

The translucent bowl separator makes it easy to add designer color treatments that complement your tiered cake. Simply fill it with fresh or silk flowers, tulle or patterned fabric, or use it on its own. The curving, fluted design adds a fresh new element that works for a variety of wedding and shower cakes. Setup couldn't be simpler: the included separator plates are spiked to fit inside the top and bottom openings of the bowl for a secure presentation. Set includes 4 in. high fluted bowl and 2 smooth-edge separator plates (6 and 10 in. diameter). Holds cakes up to 9 in. diameter.
303-823

Spiral Separator Sets

Add an elegant touch to your special occasion cakes with these beautifully scrolled separators. The curling, openwork design in white coated metal gives cakes a light, garden style design. Setup couldn't be simpler—the smooth-edge plates are spiked to fit inside the top and bottom rings for a secure presentation. Use sets together for a high-rising construction of 3 separated tiers or use on their own to hold 2 or 3 stacked tiers.

14 in. Set includes $10^1/2$ x $4^1/4$ in. high metal separator ring, 2 smooth-edge separator plates, 10 and 14 in. diameter. Holds round cakes 12 in. or smaller.
303-8175

10 in. Set includes 7 x $4^1/4$ in. high metal separator ring, 2 smooth-edge separator plates, 8 and 10 in. diameter. Holds 6, 8 or 9 in. round cakes.
303-8176

Globe Pillar and Base Sets

Sophisticated pearl-look globes separate tiered cakes for a dramatic new look. The 2 and $2^1/2$ in. Pillar Sets are positioned between tiers, as globes fit over hidden pillars to provide strong support. The 3 in. Base Set features a reinforced center channel which fits over separator plate spikes to hold your base cake. Use all three sets together to create a towering 3-tier display (see inset above). The Globe Base Set is to be used under the bottom tier only; Pillar Sets will not support the base tier.
Each set includes four globes and four 9 in. pillars, no pillars on Base Set.
2 in. **303-822 Set/8**
$2^1/2$ in. **303-824 Set/8**
3 in. Globe Base Set **303-825 Set/4**

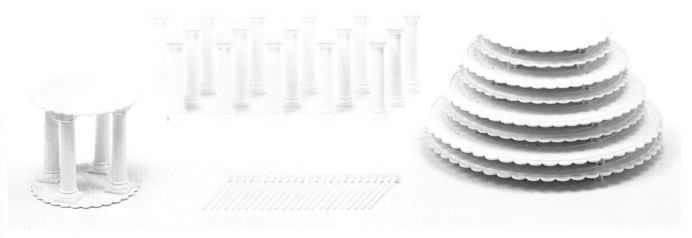

Grecian Pillar and Plate Set

A deluxe money-saving collection for the serious cake decorator. Decorator Preferred® scalloped-edge separator plates and 5 in. pillars. Includes 54 pieces: two each 6 in., 8 in., 10 in., 12 in. and 14 in. plates; 20 Grecian pillars and 24 pegs. **301-8380**

Cake Assembly Sets

Arched Tier Set

Dramatic when used with Kolor-Flo Fountain (sold on pg. 120), includes 14 pieces: Six 13 in. arched columns, two 18 in. round Decorator Preferred® separator plates and 6 angelic cherubs to attach to columns with royal icing or glue. **301-1982**

Roman Column Tier Set

Stately Roman pillars and scalloped plates create beautiful settings for all tiered cakes. Includes 8 pieces: six 13¾ in. Roman columns and 2 super strong 18 in. round Decorator Preferred® separator plates. Sized to fit with the Kolor-Flo Fountain (sold on pg. 120). **301-1981**

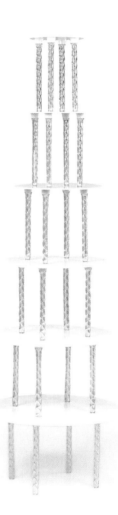

Crystal-Clear Cake Divider Set

- Sparkling clear twist legs beautifully accent your cake
- Designed for towering cakes from 6 to 14 in. diameter
- An elegant combination with Wilton Crystal-Look accessories

Clear plastic twist legs penetrate cake, rest on plate (dowel rods not needed.) Includes 6, 8, 10, 12, 14 and 16 in. plastic separator plates plus 24 legs, 7½ in. high.

301-9450 Set/30
Additional Plates

6 in.	**302-9730**
8 in.	**302-9749**
10 in.	**302-9757**
12 in.	**302-9765**
14 in.	**302-9773**
16 in.	**302-9780**

7½ in. Twist Legs 303-9794 Pk./4
9 in. Twist Legs
Add more height to your tiers.
303-977 Pk./4

Separator Pillars

Roman Columns

Handsome pillars may be used with 16 and 18 in. plates to accommodate the Kolor-Flo Fountain (sold on pg. 120).

10¼ in.	**303-8136 Pk./2**
13¾ in.	**303-2130 Pk./2**

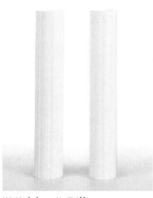

"Hidden" Pillars

Separate cake tiers slightly and create a floating illusion. Pushed into tiers as dowel rods, they fit onto all white separator plates except Tall Tier. Trimmable, hollow plastic. 6 in. high.
303-8 Pk./4

Grecian Spiked Pillars

Single plate pillars. Wide base for increased stability.

5 in.	**303-3708 Pk./4**
7 in.	**303-3710 Pk./4**
9 in.	**303-3712 Pk./4**

Grecian Pillars

Elegantly scrolled and ribbed.

3 in.	**303-3606 Pk./4**
5 in.	**303-3703 Pk./4**
7 in.	**303-3705 Pk./4**

Separator Pillars

Arched Pillars
Grecian-inspired with arched support.

4½ in.	**303-452**	Pk./4
6½ in.	**303-657**	Pk./4
13 in.	**303-9720**	Pk./2

Wrapped Pillars
Traditional 4 in. high pillars are wrapped with beautifully-textured fabric, providing an elegant new decorating option for tiered cakes.

Embroidered	**303-980**	Pk./4
Silver Lamé	**303-981**	Pk./4
Dotted	**303-982**	Pk./4

Curved Pillars
See what flair their sleek lines can bring to so many classic tiered cake designs.

2½ in.	**303-658**	Pk./4
5 in.	**303-659**	Pk./4

Separator Plates

Decorator Preferred® Scalloped Plates
Our classic scalloped-edge separator plates with superior stability and beauty. Guaranteed non-breakable.

6 in.	**302-6**	10 in.	**302-10**	14 in.	**302-14**		
7 in.	**302-7**	11 in.	**302-11**	15 in.	**302-15**		
8 in.	**302-8**	12 in.	**302-12**	16 in.	**302-16**		
9 in.	**302-9**	13 in.	**302-13**	18 in.	**302-18**		

Decorator Preferred® Smooth-Edge Plates
A fresh, clean shape which puts all the focus on your beautiful cake. Built for unmatched stability, with our patented Circles of Strength™ design. Plate feet fit securely on Wilton pillars, available in many styles. Guaranteed non-breakable.

6 in.	**302-4101**	12 in.	**302-4104**	16 in.	**302-4106**
8 in.	**302-4102**	14 in.	**302-4105**	18 in.	**302-4107**
10 in.	**302-4103**				

Square Separator Plates

7 in.	**302-1004**	11 in.	**302-1047**
9 in.	**302-1020**	13 in.	**302-1063**

Decorator Preferred® Heart Separator Plates
Perfectly sized to fit Wilton heart pans, for a stunning tiered heart creation. Guaranteed non-breakable.

8 in.	**302-60**	14 in.	**302-63**
10 in.	**302-61**	16 in.	**302-64**
12 in.	**302-62**	18 in.	**302-65**

Cake Stands

Stunning Wilton Cake Stands are the perfect way to display your special wedding cake. Take a look—there's one perfectly suited to your wedding cake size and design.

Ceramic Pedestal Cake Stand

Present your cake with elegance on this classic stand. Its fired white ceramic design features a gracefully sculpted base and a smooth attached 12 in. plate. Also use it to serve pies, brownies, cookies, candies and other special desserts. Holds cakes up to 10 in. diameter; stand is 4 in. high. **307-873**

3-Tier Cake and Dessert Stand

• Beautiful cascading effect with display platforms at 6, 12 and 19 inches high
• Holds cakes up to 8, 10 and 12 in. diameter
• Can also be used to serve appetizers, cookies and candies

Raise your party cakes, petits fours, appetizers and more to dramatic heights. With this 3-Tier Cake and Dessert Stand, creating an elegant tiered display is easier than ever! Set up is easy—the unique design combines the ease of a lightweight foam base and 3 foam support plates with the strength and dependability of 3 grooved pillars. Also included are 3 plastic plates with rings on the bottom to insure exact orientation during set-up. **304-8275**

Floating Tiers Cake Stand Sets

• Dramatic illusion of decorated tiers suspended in mid-air
• Back support ideal for adding floral or ribbon treatments
• Great for modest size weddings

Heart

Perfectly sized to heart shaped tiers. Set includes 17 in. high enamel coated white metal stand plus 8, 12 and 16 in. Decorator Preferred® removable Heart separator plates; instructions.

307-872 Set/4
Replacement Plates
8 in.	**302-60**
12 in.	**302-62**
16 in.	**302-64**

Round

Round plates present beautiful tiers. Set includes 17 in. high enamel coated white metal stand plus 8, 12, and 16 in. smooth removable separator plates; instructions.

307-825 Set/4
Replacement Plates
(Same plates as Crystal-Clear Cake Divider Set p.116)
8 in.	**302-9749**
12 in.	**302-9765**
16 in.	**302-9780**

Candlelight Cake Stand

• The magic of candlelight heightens the beauty of your cake
• Swirls of scrollwork and hearts add romance
• Great size for smaller weddings

Simple, graceful design in enameled metal is reinforced with a crossbar for more support. Holds up to 40 lbs. Ideal for three stacked tiers supported by a 14 in. separator plate. Stand is 21¹/₂ in. diameter (13¹/₂ in. center cake area) x 5 in. high. Uses standard ⁷/₈ in. candles. (Plates and candles not included.) 307-871

Tall Tier Cake Stand Set

Display your multi-tiered cakes up to 6 tiers high using this majestic stand. Lace-look plates enhance every cake design and hold tiers from 6 to 16 in. diameter. Easier to assemble than pillar construction, the twist-together center columns and strong, interchangeable plates provide sure stability. The optional Lady Windemere-Look 4-Arm Base, sold below, lets you surround up to 3 tiers with multiple small cakes for an even more dramatic presentation.

Basic Set
Includes: 5 twist-apart columns, 6½ in. high; top nut and bottom bolt; 18 in. footed base plate; 8, 10, 12, 14 and 16 in. separator plates (interchangeable, except footed base plate). Plastic.
304-7915 Set/13

Replacement Parts
Top Column Cap Nut	Bottom Column Bolt
304-7923	**304-7941**

Additional Plates
8 in.	**302-7894**	14 in.	**302-7940**
10 in.	**302-7908**	16 in.	**302-7967**
12 in.	**302-7924**	18 in.	**302-7983**

Additional Columns
6½ in.	**303-7910**	7¾ in.	**304-5009**
13½ in.	**303-703**		

Glue-On Plate Legs
Convert 14 or 16 in. separator plate into a footed base plate. Order 6 legs for each plate. **304-7930**

Cake Corer Tube (not shown)
Essential tool easily and neatly removes center from cake tiers for use with tall tier stand columns. Ice cake before using. Serrated edge removes cake center with one push. Cleans easily. **304-8172**

Lady Windemere-Look 4-Arm Base
(For Use With Tall-Tier Stand)

Easily add 4 base cakes to your tall tier cake. The 4-arm base can be used with any plate from the basic set, except the 18 in. footed base plate. Up to 3 graduated tiers can be added to the center columns. Includes 20 in. diameter 4-arm base with 4 stability pegs and base bolt. Use with 13½ in. column, bottom column bolt and four 12 in. plates, sold at left as well as the Tall Tier Basic Set. **304-8245** Additional Base Bolt **304-8253**

Garden Cake Stand
Our beautiful Garden Cake Stand echoes the wrought-iron look found in many formal gardens. Simply place cakes on plates and set on the stand. Painted metal stand is 23 in. high x 22 in. wide. Use with Decorator Preferred (Scalloped) 10 in., 14 in. and 18 in. separator plates. Satellite garden stands sold individually below. **307-860**

Satellite Garden Cake Stand
Painted metal; holds 12 in. separator plate. **307-861**

Cake Boards and Accents

Cake Circles
Corrugated cardboard for strength and stability.

6 in. diameter	2104-64 Pk./10
8 in. diameter	2104-80 Pk./12
10 in. diameter	2104-102 Pk./12
12 in. diameter	2104-129 Pk./8
14 in. diameter	2104-145 Pk./6
16 in. diameter	2104-160 Pk./6

Cake Boards
Shaped cakes look best on boards cut to fit! Strong corrugated cardboard, generously-sized in rectangular shapes. Perfect for sheet and square cakes. For shaped cakes, use the pan as a pattern and cut out board to fit cake.

10 x 14 in.	2104-554 Pk./6
13 x 19 in.	2104-552 Pk./6

Silver Cake Bases
Convenient ½ in. thick silver-covered bases are grease-resistant, food-safe and reusable. Strong to hold heavy decorated cakes without an additional serving plate. Perfect for all types of cakes and craft creations.

10 in. diameter	2104-1187 Pk./2
12 in. diameter	2104-1188 Pk./2
14 in. diameter	2104-1189 Pk./2
16 in. diameter	2104-1190 Pk./2

Fanci-Foil Wrap
Serving side has a non-toxic grease-resistant surface. FDA-approved for use with food. Continuous roll: 20 in. x 15 ft.

White	804-191
Gold	804-183
Silver	804-167

Fountains and Accessories

Kolor-Flo Fountain

Professional quality fountain makes your tiered cake design even more spectacular. Water cascades dramatically from three levels; simply remove top levels for smaller fountain arrangements. Intricate light system has two bulbs for added brilliance. Use with 14 in. or larger plates, 13 in. or taller pillars for tallest cascade. Plastic fountain bowl is 9¾ in. diameter. 110-124V, AC motor with 65 in. cord. Pumps water electrically. Directions, replacement part information included.
306-2599

Cascade Set for Kolor-Flo Fountain

Dome shapes redirect water over surface in non-stop streams. Set includes 4 pieces: 2½, 4½, 8, and 11½ in. diameter. Plastic.
306-1172 Set/4

Fanci Fountain

Economical fountain in crystal-clear design enhances any tiered cake. Adjustable, smooth water flow. Use with 14 in. or larger plates. Set-up instructions included. Height: 12 in. Diameter: 10 in. **306-2000**

Floral Accessories

Flower Holder Ring

Put at base of Kolor-Flo Fountain to surround with fresh or silk flowers. Must be placed on an 18 in. Decorator Preferred® scalloped-edge plate. 12½ in. diameter x 2 in. high. 1¾ in. wide opening; inside ring diameter is 8½ in. Plastic. **305-435**

Crystal-Look Bowl

4½ in. diameter. 1½ in. deep.
205-1404

Flower Spikes

Fill with water, push into cake, add flowers. Makes cakes safe for insertion of stems or wires. 3 in. high.
1008-408 Pk./12

Fresh Flower Holder

Insert easily under cake tiers to hold blooms, greenery, pearl sprays, tulle puffs and more. Use with floral oasis to keep flowers fresh.
205-8500 Pk./2

Dowel Rods and Pegs

Plastic Dowel Rods

Heavy-duty hollow plastic provides strong, sanitary support for all tiered cakes. Cut with serrated knife to desired length. Length: 12¾ in. Diameter: ¾ in.
399-801 Pk./4

Wooden Dowel Rods

Cut and sharpen with strong shears and knife. Length: 12 in. Diameter: ¼ in.
399-1009 Pk./12

Plastic Pegs

Insure that cake layers and separator plates atop cakes stay in place. Pegs do not add support; dowel rod cake properly before using. Length: 4 in.
399-762 Pk./12

White Pearl Beading

Molded on one continuous 5-yard strand. Remove before cutting and serving cake.
Small (4 mm) **211-1989**
Large (6 mm) **211-1990**

Wedding Figurines

More brides choose Wilton figurines to top their wedding cakes. The rich, sculpted crafting, realistic detailing and romantic designs make these figurines perfect wedding day keepsakes.

Bianca
Height: 5½ in. Base: 3¾ x 3½ in. Resin. **202-207**

Clear Bianca
Height: 5½ in. Base: 3¾ x 3½ in. Acrylic. Perfect on Lighted Revolving Base (sold on p. 122). **202-424**

Classic Couple
Reminiscent of the bride and groom that adorned wedding cake tops of years ago, this figurine adds a touch of nostalgia and retro design to your wedding celebration. Plastic. Height: 4½ in. Base: 2 x 3 in. **202-1422**

Elegance
Height: 5½ in. Base: 5 x 3 in. Resin. **110-863**

Our Day
Height: 4¾ in. Base: 2 x 1¾ in. Poly resin.

Blonde/White Gown **202-409**
Brunette/Ivory Gown (not shown) **202-415**

Love's Duet
Height: 6 in. Base: 2½ x 2¼ in. Poly resin. **202-402**

Our First Dance
Height: 9¼ in. Base: 4⅝ in. diameter. **118-650**
Couple Only Height: 6 in. Poly resin. **202-411**

Simple Joys
Height: 8 in. Base: 4½ in. diameter. **103-150**

Just Married
Height: 5 in. Base: 5 x 3½ in. Resin. **110-864**

Reflections
Porcelain couple.
Height: 8 in. Base: 4¾ in. diameter. **117-268**

Spring Song
Height: 9½ in. Base: 4⅝ in. diameter. **111-2802**
Kissing Lovebirds
5½ in. high. **1002-206**

Devotion
Height: 7 in. Base: 4 x 2½ in. Ceramic. **111-2803**

Wedding Figurines

Inspirational Cross
Height: 5¹/₂ in.
Base: 2 x 1¹/₂ in. Resin. **202-206**

Now I Have You
Height: 4¹/₄ in. Base: 4¹/₄ x 3³/₄ in.
Resin. **115-101**

Oh No You Don't
Height: 4¹/₄ in. Base: 6 x 3 in. Resin.
115-102

Lighted Revolving Base
Select just light, just rotate or both at the same time. Uses 3 AA batteries (not included). Height: 2 in.
Diameter: 5 in. **201-453**

Specialty Toppers

Monogram Picks
Stunning silver-plated pick for cake tops, floral arrangements, bouquets, and centerpieces. Use individually or in groups. Beautifully appointed with rhinestones. Food safe picks are 5 in. high including 2¹/₂ in. letters.

Available letters:

A Monogram	1008-753	J Monogram	1008-735
B Monogram	1008-755	K Monogram	1008-751
C Monogram	1008-760	L Monogram	1008-750
D Monogram	1008-732	M Monogram	1008-759
E Monogram	1008-737	P Monogram	1008-734
F Monogram	1008-736	R Monogram	1008-752
G Monogram	1008-733	S Monogram	1008-757
H Monogram	1008-754	W Monogram	1008-761

Petite 50th Ornament
Height: 5³/₄ in. Base: 4⁵/₈ in. diameter.
102-223

Anniversary Picks
Proudly display the number of years married! Appointed with rhinestones, a sparkling pick makes a beautiful keepsake for the honored couple. Use as a cake topper and in floral arrangements, bouquets, and centerpieces. Food safe. Approximately 5¹/₄ in. high.

Silver 25th
Silver plated. **1008-758**

Gold 50th
Gold plated. **1008-762**

6¹/₂ in. Cake Bow
Perfect for all celebrations—showers, weddings, birthdays! Clever cake topper can also be used as a center-piece, and may be colored to match your celebration with Wilton Icing Colors and/or royal icing. Food-safe, non-edible, paper clay. **120-1103**

12 in. Floral Cake Decorations
Beautiful, realistic white roses are so versatile for decorating your tiered cake. Use them as is or color them to match any special celebration—wedding, baby shower, graduation, anniversary or holiday. Easy to tint using non-toxic pastel chalk; complete instructions on the package. Includes three 12 in. floral lengths suitable for any size or shape cake; attach with enclosed picks or with dots of icing. Food-safe paper clay.
120-1105 Pk./3

ORDER ONLINE: WWW.WILTON.COM

Wedding Style

Timeless Ensemble
Beautiful woven satin ribbon design.
Flower Basket 120-604
Ring Bearer Pillow 120-101
Guest Pen 120-831
Guest Book 120-829
Complete Set of 4 120-460

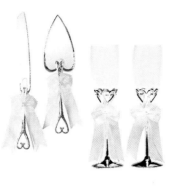

Heart Silver Toasting Glasses and Servers Ensemble
For toasting the bride and groom and cutting the cake. Elegant silver-plated heart design, organza ribbon and pearl trim. Silver plated; 10 in. high. Engrave for a beautiful keepsake.
120-232 Set/4

Pearl Toasting Glasses
Beautiful stemware to use at the reception, then at home.
Height: 9$1/2$ in.
120-783 Set/2

Graceful Toasting Glasses
Height: 10$1/2$ in.
120-716 Set/2

Crystal Look Servers
Stainless steel blades with acrylic handles.
120-4003 Set/2

Silver Candleholder Set
Keepsake-quality set holds the unity candle and tapers for the candle lighting ceremony, then adds the romantic glow of candlelight to your reception table. Silver-plated metal with ribbon trim. Unity candleholder is 6$1/4$ in. high; holds a pillar candle up to 3$3/4$ in. diameter. Each taper candleholder is 5$1/2$ in. high; holds standard size tapers. Candles not included. **120-448 Set/3**

French Rose Wedding Bouquet
Perfect, beautiful blooms to keep or to use for the bouquet toss. Handcrafted, fine silk flowers with wrapped stem. Bouquet measures approx. 8$1/2$ in. diameter with 4 in. stem. **120-1013**

Flower Petals
Fill the flower girl's basket, scatter on the cake table, decorate favors. Lifelike 2$1/2$ in. diameter flower petals. Approx. 300 petals in pack.
White Rose   **1006-698**
Red Rose   **1006-695**

Autograph Mat
Insert into your 11 x 14 in. frame to hold a 5 x 7 in. photo. Includes black pen. **1009-508**

Table Accents

Sparkling Ice
Adds sparkle to centerpieces, reception tables. Container size: 1¹/₂ in. high x 4¹/₂ in. diameter.
1006-342
WARNING: CHOKING HAZARD–Small parts. Not intended for children. Not a toy–for decorative use only.

Reception Gift Card Holder
Attractively keeps the wedding gift cards together at the reception. Tulle Spool sold separately. 7 x 12 in. high.
120-875

Celebration Tree
Use it as a party decoration, displayed on the gift table, or as a centerpiece on reception tables. Easy to assemble. Metal construction. Assembled tree measures approximately 11 x 11 x 14 in. high. (Favors and decorations shown not included.) **1006-571**

Favor Kits and Favors

25 Ct. Favor Tin Kit
Decorated tins filled with your favorite treats make the nicest favors because you personalize them to match your celebration. Simply go to www.wiltonprint.com, add your own photos, monograms or notes on the labels for your guests. Includes 25 tins, 25 printable round labels and strips, complete instructions with template information, 2 test sheets.
1006-8038 Pk./25

Goblet Favor Kit
Makes 24 favors. Includes goblet containers, tulle circles, ribbon and favor tags. **1006-923 Pk./24**

Love Knot Wands
Use after the ceremony or at the reception. 36 wands are packed in a convenient tray for reception table use. Ribbon not included. Each wand contains .16 fl. oz. bubble solution.
1007-8017 Pk./36

Wedding Bubbles
Includes 24 bottles with .6 oz. of bubbles and wands. Decorate with Tulle Circles.
1007-8000 Pk./24

Celebration Bells
Ring for a special kiss after the ceremony and at the reception. Hand to guests exiting the church or place one at each setting at the reception. Includes 24 bells, poem tags and ties. Silvertone metal bell measures 1¹/₄ in. tall.
1007-8012 Pk./24

Anniversary Bands
³/₄ in. diameter. Pk./48
Silver   **1006-101**
Gold   **1006-100**

White Sachet
Perfect for holding favors, rose petals, rice, treats, gifts.
3³/₄ x 4 in. **1006-173 Pk./12**
Also available:
4¹/₂ x 6³/₄ in. size.
1006-184 Pk./12

Tulle Circles
Sheer mesh fabric.
9 in. diameter.
1005-7897 Pk./25

Favor Accents

Add special touches to your baby favors, gift tie-ons and table decorations.

Ethnic Newborn Baby Figurines*
1 in. high. Plastic.
1103-30 Pk./6

Baby Bears*
1 in. high. Pk./6
Blue **1103-7** Pink **1103-8**
Multicolor (pink, blue, yellow, mint green.) **1103-46**

Small Safety Pins*
1½ in. long. Pk./20
Blue **1103-26** Pink **1103-21**
Multicolor (pink, blue, yellow, mint green.) **1103-42**

Mini Rocking Horses*
1¼ in. high. Pink, lavender, blue, yellow, mint green. **1103-52 Pk./6**

Newborn Baby Figurines*
1 in. high. Plastic.
1103-62 Pk./6

Decorator Icings

Ready-To-Use Decorator Icings

Wilton makes the only ready-to-use icing that is the perfect consistency for decorating. The pure white color is best for creating true vivid colors using Wilton Icing Colors. Delicious homemade taste. Certified Kosher.

5 lb. Tub—Soft & Creamy Consistency
Thin-to-medium consistency for use in Wilton Method Cake Decorating Classes in a convenient easy-carry tub. Great for spreading on cakes, making borders, messages and more. Contains 10 cups—enough to decorate 10, 8 or 9 in. round cake layers.
White **704-680**

1 lb. Can—Stiff Consistency
Ideal stiff consistency for making roses and flowers with upright petals. Contains two cups—enough to cover two 8 or 9 in. layers or one 9 x 13 in. cake.
White **710-118**
Chocolate **710-119**

Ready-To-Use Rolled Fondant

Fondant has never been more convenient and fun for decorating! With Wilton Ready-To-Use Rolled Fondant, the color is already mixed in for no kneading, no mess, no guesswork. The 24 oz. (1½ lb.) package, covers an 8 in. 2-layer cake plus decorations; the 80 oz. package (5 lbs.), available in white only, covers a 2-layer 6 in., 8 in. and 10 in. round tiered cake plus decorations. Certified Kosher.

White
24 oz. (1½ lbs.) Pk.
710-2076

White
80 oz. (5 lbs.) Pk.
710-2180

Sparkling Sugar

Put that extra dazzle in your decorating! Easy-pour sugar has a coarse texture and a brilliant sparkle that makes cupcakes, cookies and cakes really shine. 8 oz. bottle. Certified Kosher.
White. **710-992**

Candy

Perfect filler for favors, treat bags, candy dishes!

Jordan Almonds
16 oz. bag; approximately 100 pieces. Certified Kosher.
Assorted **1006-779** White **1006-778**

Pillow Mints
10 oz. bag; approximately 205 pieces. Certified Kosher.
Assorted. **1006-858**

Mint Drops
16 oz. bag. Certified Kosher.
Assorted. **1006-788**

Baby Pacifiers
12 oz. bag. Sweet/tart fruit flavor.
Assorted. **1006-540**

*WARNING: CHOKING HAZARD–Small parts. Not intended for children. Not a toy–for decorative use only.

ORDER TOLL-FREE: 800-794-5866

Decorator Preferred® Professional Aluminum Bakeware

- Straight Sides • Grip Lip Edges • Pure Aluminum
- Superior Thickness • Handcrafted Construction
- Lifetime Warranty

Our most popular bakeware—built with the most features to help decorators bake their best. Compare these benefits to any brand and discover why Decorator Preferred was rated #1 by Good Housekeeping.*

*The May 1999 Good Housekeeping Institute Report rates this Wilton Professional Pan #1 out of 31 different 9 in. round pans.

Rounds

What a selection of sizes—including the hard-to-find 18 in. Half Round, (lets you bake two halves to create one 18 in. round cake).

6 x 2 in. deep 2105-6122	12 x 2 in. deep 2105-6139	8 x 3 in. deep 2105-6105	16 x 3 in. deep 2105-6101
8 x 2 in. deep 2105-6136	14 x 2 in. deep 2105-6140	10 x 3 in. deep 2105-6104	18 x 3 in. deep Half Round 2105-6100
9 x 2 in. deep 2105-6137	16 x 2 in. deep 2105-6141	12 x 3 in. deep 2105-6103	3-Pc. Round Set 6, 10 and 14 in. diameter x 3 in. deep.
10 x 2 in. deep 2105-6138	6 x 3 in. deep 2105-6106	14 x 3 in. deep 2105-6102	2105-6114 Set/3

Sheets

Extra-thick aluminum distributes heat efficiently on these large pans.

9 x 13 x 2 in. deep	2105-6146
11 x 15 x 2 in. deep	2105-6147
12 x 18 x 2 in. deep	2105-6148

Squares

Perfect 90° corners give you the flawless look necessary for wedding tiers.

8 x 2 in. deep	2105-6142
10 x 2 in. deep	2105-6143
12 x 2 in. deep	2105-6144

Hearts

So beautiful for showers, weddings, more!

6 x 2 in. deep	2105-600
8 x 2 in. deep	2105-601
10 x 2 in. deep	2105-602
12 x 2 in. deep	2105-607
14 x 2 in. deep	2105-604
16 x 2 in. deep	2105-605

Heating Core

Distributes heat to bake large cakes evenly. Recommended for pans 10 in. diameter or larger. Releases easily from cake. $3^1/_2$ x $3^1/_2$ x 4 in. diameter.
417-6100

Performance Pans™

The classic aluminum pans—durable, even-heating and built to hold their shape through years of use. We named them Performance Pans because they perform beautifully. These are great all-purpose pans. You'll use them for casseroles, entrees, baked desserts and more. Wilton has sold millions of Performance Pans because decorators and bakers know they can depend on them.

Squares

6 x 2 in. deep	507-2180
8 x 2 in. deep	2105-8191
10 x 2 in. deep	2105-8205
12 x 2 in. deep	2105-8213
14 x 2 in. deep	2105-8220
6 x 2 in. deep	2105-8231

Rounds

6 x 2 in. deep	2105-2185	14 x 2 in. deep	2105-3947
8 x 2 in. deep	2105-2193	16 x 2 in. deep	2105-3963
10 x 2 in. deep	2105-2207	2-Pan Round Set	2105-7908
12 x 2 in. deep	2105-2215	9 x 2 in. deep	

Sheets

9 x 13 x 2 in. deep	2105-1308
11 x 15 x 2 in. deep	2105-158
12 x 18 x 2 in. deep	2105-182

ORDER ONLINE: WWW.WILTON.COM

Performance Pans™ Sets

These are the classic shapes every baker needs. Wilton has them in convenient graduated-size sets to help you create fabulous tiered cakes or individual cakes in exactly the size you want. Quality aluminum holds its shape for years. Each pan is 2 in. deep, except where noted.

Heart Pan Set

Create the ultimate tiered heart cake—a beautiful way to celebrate showers, weddings and more. Now redesigned for a perfect fit when used with our Decorator Preferred Heart Separator Plates shown on page 116. Includes 6, 10, 12 and 14 in. pans.
2105-606 Set/4

Round Pan Set
Includes 6, 8, 10, 12 in. pans.
2105-2101 Set/4

Round Pan Set, 3 in. Deep
Includes 8, 10, 12, 14 in. pans.
2105-2932 Set/4

Oval Pan Set
Includes 7³/₄ x 5⁵/₈, 10³/₄ x 7⁷/₈, 13¹/₂ x 9⁷/₈ and 16¹/₂ x 12³/₈ in. pans.
2105-2130 Set/4

Square Pan Set
Includes 8, 12, 16 in. pans.
2105-2132 Set/3

Hexagon Pan Set
Includes 6, 9, 12, 15 in. pans.
2105-3572 Set/4

Petal Pan Set
Includes 6, 9, 12, 15 in. pans.
2105-2134 Set/4

Novelty Shaped Pans

3-D Rubber Ducky Pan
This bath-time favorite will make the biggest splash for birthdays, baby showers and school celebrations. Five adorable decorating ideas included. Two-piece pan takes 5¹/₂ cups of firm-textured batter, 9 x 5 x 7 in. high. Aluminum.
2105-2094

Sports Ball Pan Set
Use this four-piece set to create a perfect sports cake centerpiece. Includes two 6 in. diameter half-ball pans and two metal baking stands. Each pan half takes 2¹/₂ cups of firm-textured batter. Aluminum.
2105-6506 Set/4

Mini Ball Pan
Ice two mini balls and push together for a 3-D effect. One cake mix makes 10-12 mini balls. Six cavities, each 3¹/₂ x 3¹/₂ x 1¹/₂ in. deep. Aluminum.
2105-1760

Stand-Up Cuddly Bear Set
Five decorating ideas on the box! Two-piece pan takes 6²/₃ cups of firm textured batter. Includes 6 clips, heat-conducting core and instructions. Pan is 9 x 6³/₄ x 8⁵/₈ in. high. Aluminum.
2105-603 Set/10

There's always something new at Wilton! Fun decorating courses that will help your decorating skills soar. Exciting cake designs to challenge you. Great new decorating products to try. Helpful hints to make your decorating more efficient and successful. Here's how you can keep up to date with what's happening at Wilton.

Decorating Classes

Do you want to learn more about cake decorating, with the personal guidance of a Wilton instructor? Wilton has two ways to help you.

The Wilton School of Cake Decorating and Confectionery Art is the home of the world's most popular cake decorating system—The Wilton Method.

For more than 75 years, thousands of students from around the world have learned to decorate cakes using the techniques featured in The Wilton Method. In 1929, Dewey McKinley Wilton taught the first small classes in the kitchen of his Chicago home. Today, The Wilton School teaches more people to decorate than any school in the world. As the school has grown, some techniques have been refined and there are more classes to choose from—but the main philosophies of the Wilton Method have remained.

The Wilton School occupies a state-of-the-art facility in Darien, Illinois. More than 90 courses are offered each year, including The Master Course, a 2-week class that provides individualized instruction in everything from borders and flowers to constructing a tiered wedding cake. Other courses focus on specific decorating subjects, such as Lambeth and Cakes for Catering. Courses in Gum Paste and Chocolate Artistry feature personal instruction from well-known experts in the field.

For more information or to enroll, write to:
Wilton School of Cake Decorating and Confectionery Art
2240 West 75th Street, Woodridge, IL 60517
Attn: School Coordinator

Or call: 630-810-2211 for a free brochure and schedule.

Wilton Method Classes are the convenient way to learn to decorate, close to your home. Our classes are easy and fun for everyone. You can learn the fundamentals of cake decorating with a Wilton-trained teacher in just four 2-hour classes. When the course is over, you'll know how to decorate star and shell birthday cakes or floral anniversary cakes like a pro. Everyone has a good time—it's a great place for new decorators to discover their talent. Since 1974, hundreds of thousands have enjoyed these courses.

Special Project Classes are also available in subjects like candy-making, gingerbread, fondant, cookie blossoms and more.

Call 800-942-8881 for class locations and schedules.

Wilton Products

Visit a Wilton Dealer near you. Your local Wilton Dealer is the best place to see the great variety of cake decorating products made by Wilton. If you are new to decorating, it's a good idea to see these products in person; if you are an experienced decorator, you'll want to visit your Wilton Dealer regularly to have the supplies you need on hand. From bakeware and icing supplies to candles and publications, most Wilton retailers carry a good stock of items needed for decorating. Remember, the selection of products changes with each season, so if you want to decorate cakes in time for upcoming holidays, visit often to stock up on current pans, colors and toppers.

Order on-line, by phone or by mail. You can also place orders 24 hours a day at our website, www.wilton.com. Shopping on-line is fast, easy and secure. Or, you can place an order by phone at 800-794-5866 (7WILTON) or by mail, using the Order Form in the Wilton Yearbook of Cake Decorating.

Wilton On The Web

www.wilton.com is the place to find Wilton decorating information on-line. Looking for a fun new cake to make? Our website is filled with great decorating ideas, updated regularly to fit the season. Need a recipe? *www.wilton.com* has delicious desserts and icings to try. Want to save decorating time? There are always helpful hints and answers to common decorating questions. You can also discover new Wilton products and shop for your favorites at *www.wilton.com*.

Wilton Publications

We never run out of decorating ideas! Each year, Wilton publishes more new idea books based on Wilton Method techniques. When you're planning a specific occasion, Wilton books are a fantastic source of decorating inspiration.

The Wilton Yearbook of Cake Decorating is our annual showcase of the latest ideas in decorating. Each edition is packed with all-new cake ideas, instructions and products—it's the best place to find out what's new at Wilton. Cakes for every occasion throughout the year are here: holidays, graduations, birthdays, weddings and more. If you are looking for a new cake to test your decorating skills, you can't beat the Yearbook.

Wilton also regularly publishes special interest decorating books, including books on wedding and holiday decorating, candy-making, home entertaining and food gifting. Look for them wherever Wilton products are sold.